ITALIAN

in 10 minutes a day®

by **Kristine Kershul,** M.A., University of California, Santa Barbara

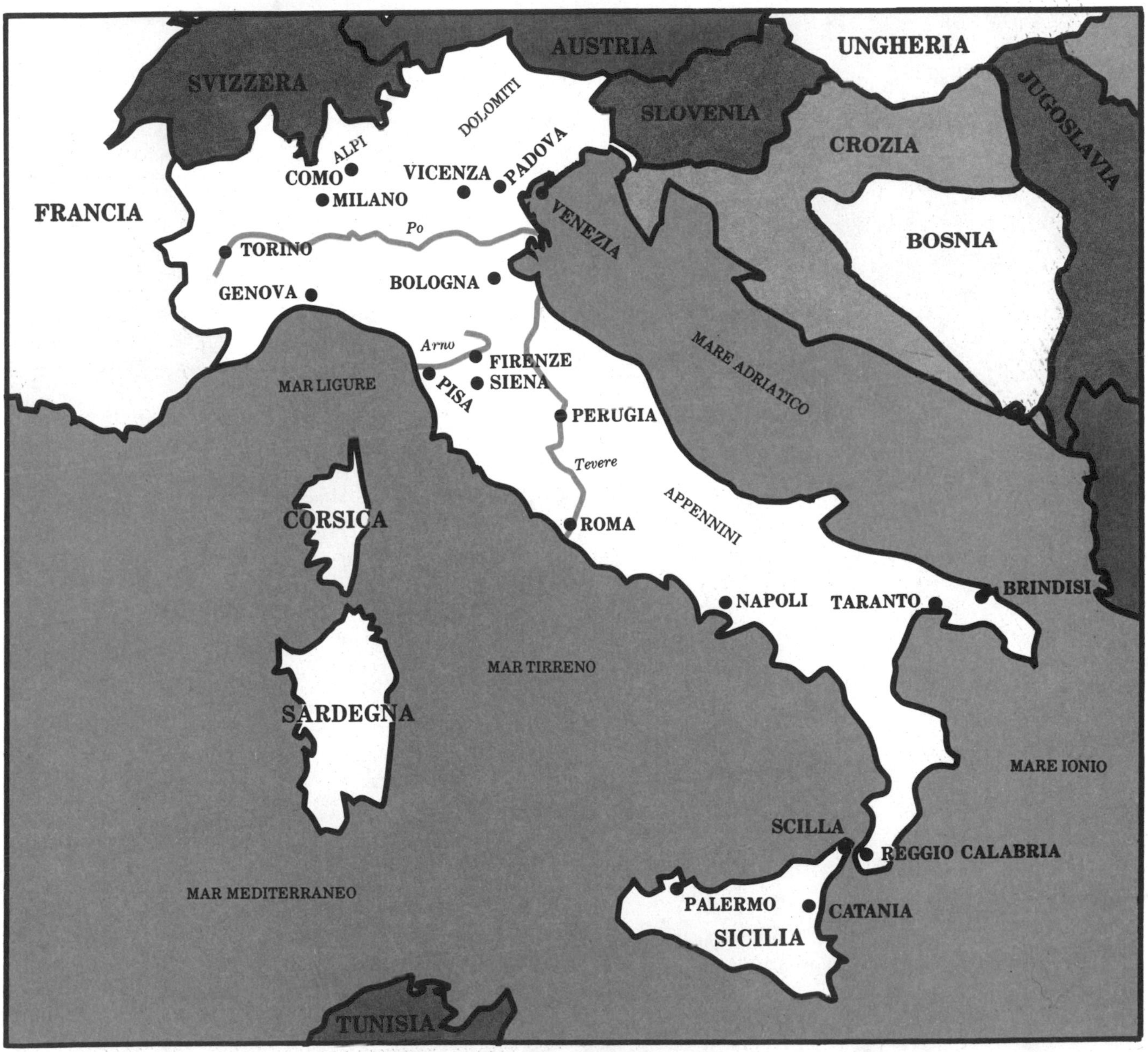

Bilingual Books Inc.
511 Eastlake Avenue E., Seattle, WA 98109
Tel: (206) 340-4422 Fax: (206) 340-9816

Fifth printing July 1995

 ISBN 0-944502-55-5.

(lahl-fah-beh-toh)

L'alfabeto

Many Italian letters sound the same as they do in English, but some Italian letters are pronounced or written **differently. To learn the Italian sounds of these letters,** write each example in the space provided, in addition to **saying each word many times. After you practice the word,** see if you can locate it on the map.

Italian letter	English sound	Example	(Write it here)
a	ah	**Catania** *(kah-tah-nee-ah)*	
c *(before a,o,u and all consonants)*	k	**Como** *(koh-moh)*	
ch	k	**Marche** *(mahr-keh)*	Marche
c *(before e,i)*	ch	**Sicilia** *(see-chee-lee-ah)*	
ci *(before a,o,u)*	ch	**Francia** *(frahn-chah)*	
e	eh *(as in let)*	**Tevere** *(teh-veh-reh)*	
g *(before a,o,u)*	g *(as in go)*	**Garda** *(gahr-dah)*	
gh	g *(as in spaghetti)*	**Alleghe** *(ahl-leh-geh)*	
g *(before e,i)*	j *(as in John)*	**Genova** *(jeh-noh-vah)*	
gi *(before a,o,u)*	j *(as in John)*	**Reggio** *(reh-joh)*	
gli	l-y *(as in million)*	**Puglia** *(pool-yah)*	
gn	n-y *(as in onion)*	**Bologna** *(boh-lohn-yah)*	
i	ee	**Pisa** *(pee-sah)*	
o	oh	**Po** *(poh)*	
r	*(slightly rolled)*	**Roma** *(roh-mah)*	
s *(beginning a word and followed by a consonant)*	z	**Svizzera** *(zvee-tseh-rah)*	
sc *(before a,o,u)*	sk	**Toscana** *(toh-skah-nah)*	
sch *(before e,i)*	sk	**Ischia** *(ee-skee-ah)*	
sc *(before e,i)*	sh	**Scilla** *(sheel-lah)*	Scilla
sci *(before a,o,u)*	sh	**Brescia** *(breh-shah)*	
s *(all other cases)*	s	**Siena** *(see-eh-nah)*	
u	oo	**Umbria** *(oom-bree-ah)*	
z *(varies)*	ts	**Venezia** *(veh-neh-tsee-ah)*	
	z	**Vicenza** *(vee-chehn-zah)*	

Vowels are easy! They are always pronounced the same. "a" is always "ah," "e" is always "eh," "i" is always "ee," "o" is always "oh," and "u" will always be "oo." "h" is never pronounced.

Seven Key Question Words

When you arrive in (ee-tah-lee-ah) **Italia,** the very first thing you will need to do is to ask questions — "Where is the train station?" "Where can I exchange money?" "Where (doh-veh) **(dove)** is the lavatory?" "(doh-veh) **Dove** is the restaurant?" "(doh-veh) **Dove** do I catch a taxi?" "**Dove** is a good hotel?" "**Dove** is my luggage?" — and the list will go on and on for the entire length of your visit. In Italian, there are SEVEN KEY QUESTION WORDS to learn. For example, the seven key question words will help you find out exactly what you are ordering in a restaurant before you order it — and not after the surprise (or shock!) arrives. Take a few minutes to study and practice saying the seven basic question words listed below. Notice that "what" and "who" are differentiated by only one letter, so be sure not to confuse them. Then cover the Italian words with your hand and fill in each of the blanks with the matching (pah-roh-lah) **parola** (word) (ee-tah-lee-ah-nah) **italiana** (Italian).

1.	(doh-veh) **DOVE**	=	WHERE	dove, dove, dove
2.	(kee) **CHI**	=	WHO	________________
3.	(keh) **CHE**	=	WHAT	________________
4.	(pehr-keh) **PERCHÈ**	=	WHY	________________
5.	(kwahn-doh) **QUANDO**	=	WHEN	________________
6.	(koh-meh) **COME**	=	HOW	________________
7.	(kwahn-toh) **QUANTO**	=	HOW MUCH	________________

Now test yourself to see if you really can keep the *(pah-roh-leh)* **parole** [words] straight in your mind. Draw lines between the Italian *(eh)* **e** [and] English equivalents below.

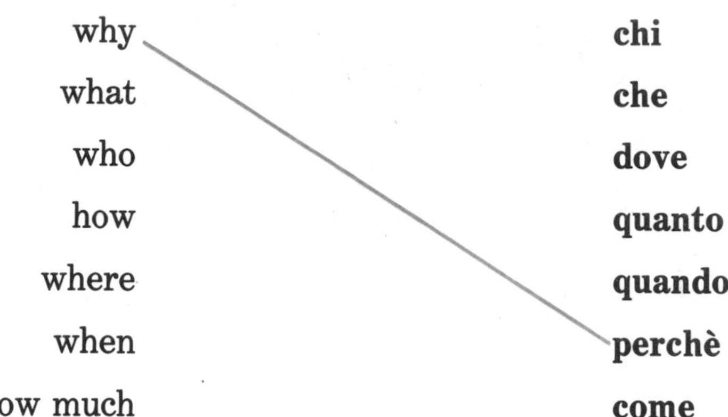

why	**chi**
what	**che**
who	**dove**
how	**quanto**
where	**quando**
when	**perchè**
how much	**come**

Examine the following questions containing these *(pah-roh-leh)* **parole.** Practice the sentences many times *(eh)* **e** [and] then quiz yourself by filling in the blanks below with the correct question *(pah-roh-lah)* **parola.** [word]

(doh-veh) (eel) (teh-leh-foh-noh)
Dov'è il telefono?
Where is the telephone?

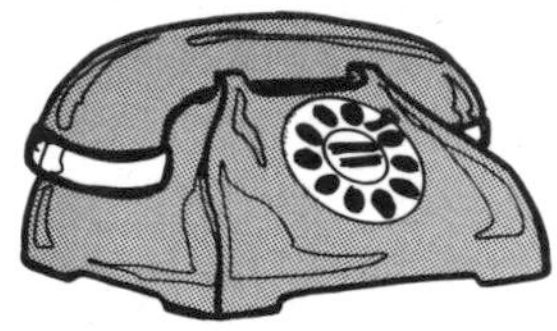

(kee) (eh)
Chi è?
Who is it?

(kwahn-toh) (eh)
Quanto è?
How much is it?

(kwahn-doh) (ahr-ree-vah) (eel) (treh-noh)
Quando arriva il treno?
When does the train arrive?

(keh) (soo-cheh-deh)
Che succede?
What's happening?

(koh-meh) (leen-sah-lah-tah)
Com'è l'insalata?
How is the salad?

(keh) (eh)
Che è?
What is it?

(pehr-keh) (nohn) (ahr-ree-vah) (eel) (seen-yoh-reh)
Perchè non arriva il signore?
Why doesn't arrive the man?

1. Com' **è l'insalata?**
2. ____________ **è?**
3. ____________ **succede?**
4. ____________ **è il telefono?**
5. ____________ **non arriva il signore?**
6. ____________ **arriva il treno?**
7. ____________ **è?**
8. ____________ **è?**

(doh-veh) **Dove** will be your most used question **parola,** so let's concentrate on it. *(ree-peh-tah)* **Ripeta** [repeat] the following Italian sentences aloud. Then write out each sentence without looking at the *(eh-sehm-pee-oh)* **esempio.** [example] If you don't succeed on the first try, don't give up. Just practice each sentence until you are able to do it easily. Don't forget that **"che"** is pronounced like "keh" and **"chi"** like "kee." Also, **"ce"** is pronounced like "cheh" and **"ci"** like "chee."

(soh-noh) (ee) (gah-bee-net-tee)
Dove sono i gabinetti?

(eel) (tahs-see)
Dov'è il tassì?

(lah-oo-toh-boos)
Dov'è l'autobus?

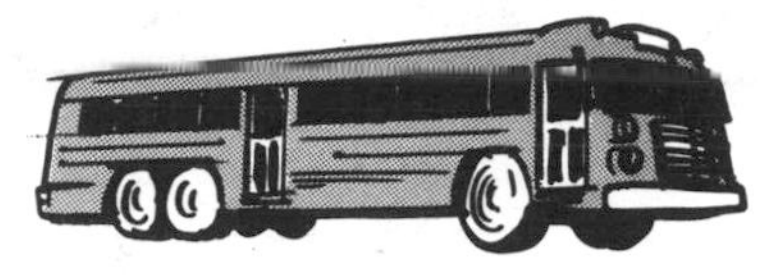

____________ *Dov'è il tassì?* ____________

(eel) (ree-stoh-rahn-teh)
Dov'è il ristorante?

(lah) (bahn-kah)
Dov'è la banca?

(lahl-behr-goh)
Dov'è l'albergo?

____________ ____________ ____________

Sí (see) (yes), many of the **parole** (pah-roh-leh) which look like **inglese** (een-gleh-seh) (English) are also **italiane** (ee-tah-lee-ah-neh) (Italian). Since **italiano** (ee-tah-lee-ah-noh) **e** (eh) **inglese** (een-gleh-seh) share many words, your work here **è** (eh) (is) simpler. You will be amazed at the number of **parole** which are **identiche** (ee-dehn-tee-keh) (identical) (or almost **identiche**). Of course, they do not always sound the same when spoken by an Italian, but the **similitudini** (see-mee-lee-too-dee-nee) (similarities) will certainly surprise you. Listed below are five "free" **parole** (pah-roh-leh) beginning with "a" to help you get started. Be sure to say each **parola** aloud **e** (eh) then write out the **parole italiane** (ee-tah-lee-ah-neh) in the blank to the right.

- ☑ **l'alcool** *(lahl-kohl)* .... alcohol __________
- ☑ **le Alpi** *(ahl-pee)* .... Alps __________
- ☑ **americano** *(ah-meh-ree-kah-noh)* .... American __________
- ☑ **l'animale** *(lah-nee-mah-leh)* .... animal *l'animale*
- ☑ **l'appartamento** *(lahp-pahr-tah-mehn-toh)* .. apartment __________

Free parole like these will appear at the bottom of the following pages in a yellow color band. They are easy — enjoy them!

Step 2

"the," "a," "some"

All of these words mean "the" in **italiano**:

(eel) **il**	(loh) **lo**	(lah) **la**	**l'**	(ee) **i**	(l-yee) **gli**	(leh) **le**

il ragazzo (rah-gah-tsoh):	the boy	**i ragazzi** (rah-gah-tsee):	the boys
l'amico (lah-mee-koh):	the friend	**gli amici** (ah-mee-chee):	the friends
lo zio (zee-oh):	the uncle	**gli zii** (zee):	the uncles
la ragazza (rah-gah-tsah):	the girl	**le ragazze** (rah-gah-tseh):	the girls

These words mean "a" or "an":

(oon) **un**	(oo-noh) **uno**	(oo-nah) **una**	(oon) **un'**

These words mean "some":

(deh-ee) **dei**	(dehl-yee) **degli**	(dehl-leh) **delle**

un signore (seen-yoh-reh):	a gentleman	**dei signori** (seen-yoh-ree):	some gentlemen
uno zaino (zah-ee-noh):	a backpack	**degli zaini** (zah-ee-nee):	some backpacks
una signora (seen-yoh-rah):	a lady	**delle signore** (seen-yoh-reh):	some ladies
un'arancia (ah-rahn-chah):	an orange	**delle arance** (ah-rahn-cheh):	some oranges

L'italiano (lee-tah-lee-ah-noh) has multiple **parole** for "the," "a" and "some," but there **è** (eh) [is] no need to worry about it. Just make a choice **e** (eh) remember to use one of these **parole**.

Step 3

Before you proceed **con** (kohn) [with] this Step, situate yourself comfortably in your living room. Now look around you. Can you name the things that you see in the **stanza** (stahn-zah) [room] in **italiano?** You can probably guess **la lampada** (lahm-pah-dah) and maybe even **il tavolo** (tah-voh-loh). But let's learn the rest of them. After practicing these **parole** out loud, write them in the blanks below **e** (eh) on the next page.

il quadro (kwah-droh) = the picture ____________________

il soffitto (sohf-fee-toh) = the ceiling ____________________

- ☐ **l'appetito** *(lahp-peh-tee-toh)* .... appetite ____________
- ☐ **aprile** *(ah-pree-leh)* .... April ____________
- ☐ **l'arrivo** *(lahr-ree-voh)* .... arrival ____________
- ☐ **l'attenzione** *(laht-tehn-tsee-oh-neh)* .... attention ____________
- ☐ **l'attore** *(laht-toh-reh)* .... actor ____________

(lahn-goh-loh)
l'angolo = the corner ______

(fee-neh-strah)
la finestra = the window ______

(lahm-pah-dah)
la lampada = the lamp ______

(loo-cheh)
la luce = the light ______

(soh-fah)
il sofà = the sofa ______

(seh-dee-ah)
la sedia = the chair ______

(tahp-peh-toh)
il tappeto = the carpet ______

(tah-voh-loh)
il tavolo = the table ______

(pohr-tah)
la porta = the door ______

(loh-roh-loh-joh)
l'orologio = the clock ______

(ten-dee-nah)
la tendina = the curtain ______

(pah-reh-teh)
la parete = the wall ______

You will notice that the correct form of **il** (eel), **la o** (oh) **l'** is given **con** (kohn) (with) each noun. This is for your **informazione** (een-fohr-mah-tsee-oh-neh) (information) — just remember to use one of them. Now open your book to the first page **con** the stick-on labels. Peel off the first 14 labels **e** (eh) proceed around the **stanza,** (stahn-zah) (room) labeling these items in your home. This will help to increase your Italian **parola** power easily. Don't forget to say **le parole** as you attach each label.

Now ask yourself, **"Dov'è il (eel) quadro?"** e point at it while you answer, **"Ecco (ehk-koh) (there is) il quadro (kwah-droh)."**

Continue on down the **lista** (lee-stah) (list) until you feel comfortable with these new **parole.** Say, **"Dov'è il (eel) soffitto (sohf-fee-toh)?"** Then **risponda,** (ree-spohn-dah) (respond) **"Ecco il soffitto,"** and so on. When you identify all the items on the **lista,** (lee-stah) you will be ready to move on.

Now, starting on the next page, let's learn some **basic parts of the house.**

- ☐ **la baia** *(bah-ee-ah)*..................... bay ______
- ☐ **il balcone** *(bahl-koh-neh)*................ balcony ______
- ☐ **la banana** *(bah-nah-nah)*.................. banana ______
- ☐ **la banca** *(bahn-kah)*..................... bank ______
- ☐ **la benedizione** *(beh-neh-dee-tsee-oh-neh)*.... benediction ______

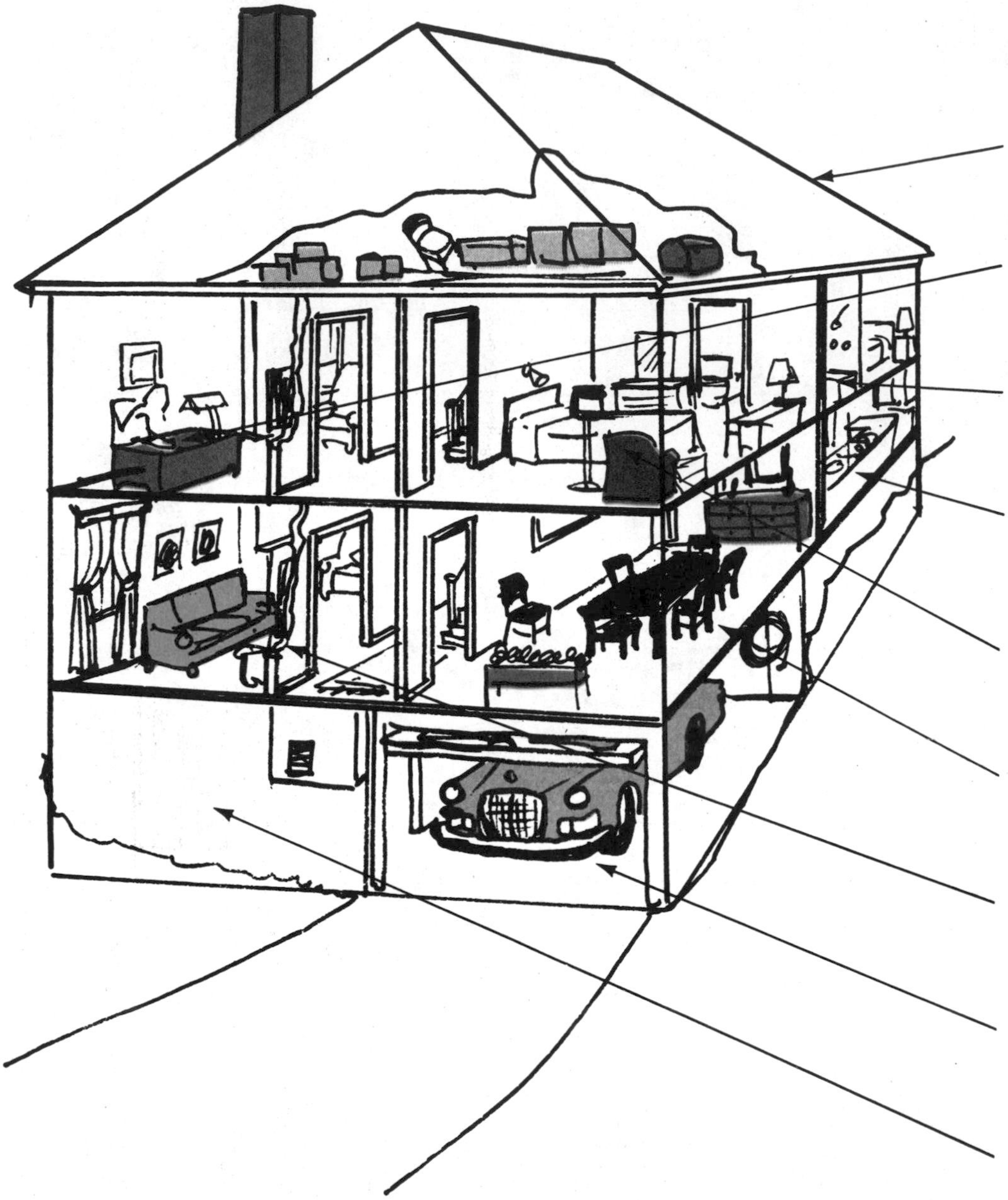

(lah)(kah-sah)
la casa = the house

(ehk-koh)
Ecco la casa.
here is

(loof-fee-choh)
l'ufficio
office

(stahn-zah) (dah) (bahn-yoh)
la **stanza da bagno**
bathroom

(koo-chee-nah)
la **cucina**
kitchen

(kah-meh-rah) (dah) (let-toh)
la **camera da letto**
bedroom

(sah-lah) (dah) (prahn-zoh)
la **sala da pranzo**
dining room

(sah-loht-toh)
il **salotto**
living room

(gah-rahzh)
il **garage**
garage

(kahn-tee-nah)
la cantina
cellar

While learning these new **parole** *(pah-roh-leh)*, let's not forget
words

(lah-oo-toh) (mahk-kee-nah)
l'auto/la macchina

(bee-chee-klet-tah)
la bicicletta

(kah-neh)
il cane

______________ ______________ *il cane*

- ☐ **il biscotto** *(bee-skoht-toh)* .... biscuit, cookie ______________
- ☐ **la bistecca** *(bee-stehk-kah)* .... beefsteak ______________
- ☐ **la bottiglia** *(boht-teel-yah)* .... bottle ______________
- ☐ **breve** *(breh-veh)* .... brief, short ______________
- ☐ **brillante** *(breel-lahn-teh)* .... brilliant, shining ______________

(gaht-toh)
il gatto

(jahr-dee-noh)
il giardino

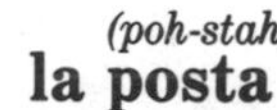

(poh-stah)
la posta

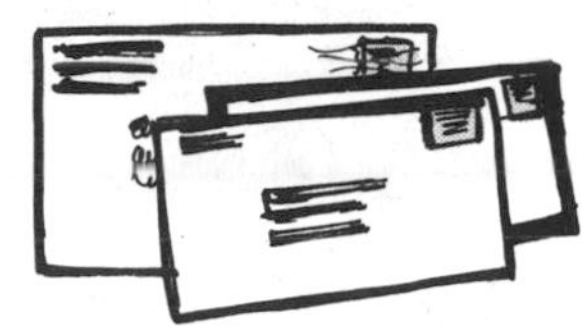

il giardino

(boo-kah) (del-leh) (let-teh-reh)
la buca delle lettere

(fee-oh-ree)
i fiori

(kahm-pah-nel-loh)
il campanello

doorbell

Peel off the next set of labels *(eh)* **e** wander through your *(kah-sah)* **casa** learning these new *(pah-roh-leh)* **parole.**

Granted, it will be somewhat difficult to label your *(kah-neh)* **cane,** *(gaht-toh)* **gatto o** *(fee-oh-ree)* **fiori,** but use your *(eem-mah-jee-nah-tsee-oh-neh)* **immaginazione.**

Again, practice by asking yourself, **"Dov'è il** *(jahr-dee-noh)* **giardino?"** e *(ree-spohn-dah)* **risponda, "Ecco il giardino."**

Dov'è ...

- ☐ **la capitale** *(kah-pee-tah-leh)* .... capital
- ☐ **il castello** *(kah-stehl-loh)* .... castle
- ☐ **la categoria** *(kah-teh-goh-ree-ah)* .... category
- ☐ **la cattedrale** *(kaht-teh-drah-leh)* .... cathedral
- ☐ **il centro** *(chehn-troh)* .... center, downtown

Step 4

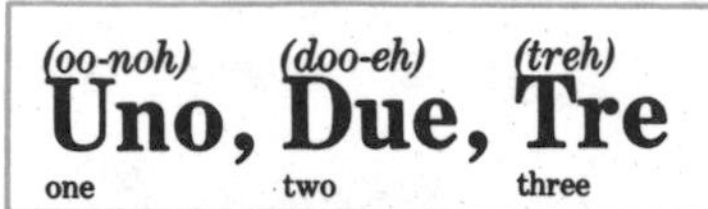

You might hear **bambini** *(bahm-bee-nee)* [children] **italiani** *(ee-tah-lee-ah-nee)* [Italian] reciting this rhyme:

> **Uno, due, tre, la** *(lah)* **Peppina** *(pehp-pee-nah)* **fa** *(fah)* **il** *(eel)* **caffè;** *(kahf-feh)*
> one two three Peppina makes the coffee
>
> **Quattro,** *(kwaht-troh)* **cinque,** *(cheen-kweh)* **sei,** *(seh-ee)* **anch'io** *(ahnk-ee-oh)* **lo** *(loh)* **vorrei.** *(vohr-reh-ee)*
> four five six also I it would like

For some reason, numbers are not the easiest thing to learn, but just remember how important they are in everyday **conversazione** *(kohn-vehr-sah-tsee-oh-neh)* [conversation]. How could you tell someone your phone number, your address or your hotel room if you had no numbers? And think of how difficult it would be if you could not understand the time, the price of an apple or the correct **autobus** *(ah-oo-toh-boos)* [bus] to take. When practicing the **numeri** *(noo-meh-ree)* [numbers] below, notice the **similitudini** *(see-mee-lee-too-dee-nee)* [similarities] between **quattro** *(kwaht-troh)* (4) and **quattordici** *(kwaht-tohr-dee-chee)* (14), **sette** *(set-teh)* (7) and **diciassette** *(dee-chahs-set-teh)* (17) **e** so on.

0	*(zeh-roh)* **zero**			0	zero, zero, zero
1	*(oo-noh)* **uno**	11	*(oon-dee-chee)* **undici**	1	
2	*(doo-eh)* **due**	12	*(doh-dee-chee)* **dodici**	2	
3	*(treh)* **tre**	13	*(treh-dee-chee)* **tredici**	3	
4	*(kwaht-troh)* **quattro**	14	*(kwaht-tohr-dee-chee)* **quattordici**	4	
5	*(cheen-kweh)* **cinque**	15	*(kween-dee-chee)* **quindici**	5	
6	*(seh-ee)* **sei**	16	*(seh-dee-chee)* **sedici**	6	
7	*(set-teh)* **sette**	17	*(dee-chahs-set-teh)* **diciassette**	7	
8	*(oht-toh)* **otto**	18	*(dee-choht-toh)* **diciotto**	8	
9	*(noh-veh)* **nove**	19	*(dee-chahn-noh-veh)* **diciannove**	9	
10	*(dee-eh-chee)* **dieci**	20	*(ven-tee)* **venti**	10	

- ☐ **la cerimonia** *(cheh-ree-moh-nee-ah)* .... ceremony ______
- ☐ **certo** *(chehr-toh)* .... certainly ______
- ☐ **il cinema** *(chee-neh-mah)* .... cinema, movie house ______
- ☐ **il cioccolato** *(chok-koh-lah-toh)* .... chocolate ______
- ☐ **la comunicazione** *(koh-moo-nee-kah-tsee-oh-neh)* communication ______

(oo-see) **Usi** (use) these *(noo-meh-ree)* **numeri** on a daily basis. Count to yourself *(een)* **in italiano** when you brush your teeth, exercise, *(oh)* **o** (or) commute to work. Now fill in the following blanks according to the **numeri** in parentheses.

Note: This is a good time to start learning these two important phrases.

(vohr-reh-ee) **vorrei**	=	I would like ________________
(vohr-rehm-moh) **vorremmo**	=	we would like ________________

(vohr-reh-ee) **Vorrei**	________ (15)	*(fohl-yee)(dee) (kahr-tah)* **fogli di carta.** pieces of paper	*(kwahn-tee)* **Quanti?**	________ (15)
Vorrei	________ (10)	*(kahr-toh-lee-neh)* **cartoline.** postcards	**Quanti?**	________ (10)
Vorrei	________ (11)	*(frahn-koh-bohl-lee)* **francobolli.** stamps	**Quanti?**	________ (11)
Vorrei	________ (8)	*(lee-tree)(dee) (behn-zee-nah)* **litri di benzina.** liters of gasoline	**Quanti?**	otto (8)
Vorrei	________ (1)	*(beek-kee-eh-reh)(dee) (ah-rahn-chah-tah)* **bicchiere di aranciata.** glass of orangeade	**Quanti?**	________ (1)
(vohr-rehm-moh) **Vorremmo**	________ (3)	*(beel-yet-tee) (ah-oo-toh-boos)* **biglietti dell'autobus** bus tickets	**Quanti?**	________ (3)
Vorremmo	________ (4)	*(tah-tseh) (dee) (teh)* **tazze di tè.** cups of tea	**Quanti?**	________ (4)
Vorremmo	due (2)	*(beer-reh)* **birre.** beers	**Quanti?**	________ (2)
Vorrei	________ (12)	*(oo-oh-vah)(freh-skeh)* **uova fresche.** eggs fresh	**Quanti?**	________ (12)
Vorremmo	________ (6)	*(kee-lee) (dee) (kahr-neh)* **chili di carne.** kilos of meat	**Quanti?**	________ (6)
Vorremmo	________ (5)	*(beek-kee-eh-ree) (dee) (vee-noh)* **bicchieri di vino.** glasses of wine	**Quanti?**	________ (5)
Vorrei	________ (7)	*(beek-kee-eh-ree) (dee) (ahk-kwah)* **bicchieri di acqua.** glasses of water	**Quanti?**	________ (7)
Vorremmo	________ (9)	*(kee-lee) (dee) (boor-roh)* **chili di burro.** kilos of butter	**Quanti?**	________ (9)

- ☐ **la conservazione** *(kohn-sehr-vah-tsee-oh-neh)* . conservation ________________
- ☐ **la conversazione** *(kohn-vehr-sah-tsee-oh-neh)* . conversation ________________
- ☐ **il coraggio** *(koh-rah-joh)* .... courage ________________
- ☐ **la cugina** *(koo-jee-nah)* .... female cousin ________________
- ☐ **il cugino** *(koo-jee-noh)* .... male cousin ________________

Now see if you can translate the following thoughts into **italiano.** *(leh)* **Le** *(ree-spoh-steh)* **risposte** (answers) are at the bottom of the *(pah-jee-nah)* **pagina.** (page)

1. I would like seven postcards.

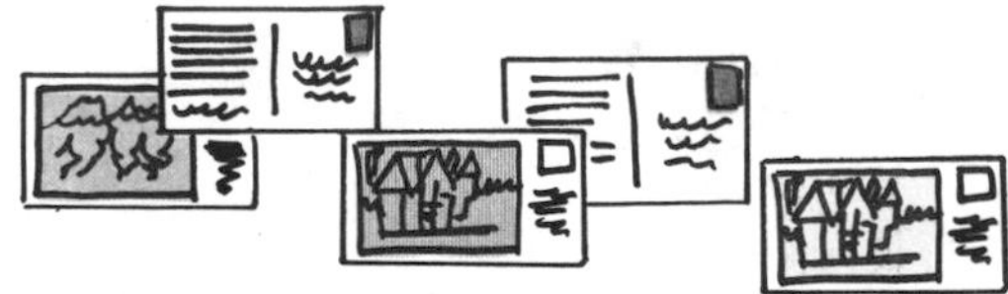

____

2. I would like one beer.

Vorrei una birra.

3. We would like two glasses of water.

____

4. We would like three bus tickets.

____

Review **i numeri** 1 *(ah)* **a** (to) 20 **e** answer the following *(doh-mahn-deh)* **domande** (questions) aloud, **e** then write the *(ree-spoh-steh)* **risposte** in the blank spaces to the left.

(kwahn-tee) **Quanti** (how many) *(tah-voh-lee)* **tavoli** *(chee)(soh-noh)* **ci sono?** (there are)

tre

Quante *(lahm-pah-deh)* **lampade** *(chee)(soh-noh)* **ci sono?**

____

Quante *(seh-dee-eh)* **sedie ci sono?**

____

RISPOSTE CORRETTE

1. **Vorrei sette cartoline.**
2. **Vorrei una birra.**
3. **Vorremmo due bicchieri di acqua.**
4. **Vorremmo due biglietti dell'autobus.**

(kwahn-tee) (oh-roh-loh-jee)(chee) (soh-noh)
Quanti orologi ci sono?
how many

(fee-neh-streh)
Quante finestre ci sono? una

(pehr-soh-neh)
Quante persone ci sono?

(seen-yoh-ree)
Quanti signori ci sono?
men

(dohn-neh)
Quante donne ci sono?
women

(koh-loh-ree) I Colori
colors

Step 5

I colori (ee) (koh-loh-ree) **sono** (soh-noh) (are) the same **in** (een) **Italia** (ee-tah-lee-ah) as **in America** (ah-meh-ree-kah) — they just have different **nomi** (noh-mee) (names). You can easily recognize **violetto** (vee-oh-leht-toh) as violet. So when you are invited to someone's **casa** (kah-sah) (house) **e** you want to bring flowers, you will be able to order the **colore corretto** (kohr-reht-toh) of flowers. (Contrary to American custom, **in** (een) **Europa** (eh-oo-roh-pah) **i fiori** (fee-oh-ree) **rossi,** (rohs-see) (red) **e** particularly **le rose** (roh-seh) (roses) **rosse,** (rohs-seh) (red) are only exchanged between lovers!) Let's learn the basic **colori.** Once you have read through **la lista** (lee-stah) on the next **pagina,** (pah-jee-nah) cover the **italiano con** (with) your **mano,** (mah-noh) (hand) **e** practice writing out the **italiano** (ee-tah-lee-ah-noh) next to the **inglese.** (een-gleh-seh) Notice the **similitudini** (see-mee-lee-too-dee-nee) between **le parole in italiano e in inglese.**

- ☐ **la danza** *(dahn-tsah)* .... dance ______
- ☐ **decorato** *(deh-koh-rah-toh)* .... decorated ______
- ☐ **delizioso** *(deh-lee-tsee-oh-soh)* .... delicious ______
- ☐ **denso** *(dehn-soh)* .... dense ______
- ☐ **il desiderio** *(deh-see-deh-ree-oh)* .... desire ______

(bee-ahn-koh) **bianco**	= white	______	*(bahr-kah) (eh)(bee-ahn-kah)* **La barca è bianca.** boat is
(neh-roh) **nero**	= black	______	*(pahl-lah) (neh-rah)* **La palla è nera.** ball
(jahl-loh) **giallo**	= yellow	______	*(bah-nah-nah) (jahl-lah)* **La banana è gialla.**
(rohs-soh) **rosso**	= red	______	*(lee-broh)* **Il libro è rosso.** book
(ah-zoor-roh) **azzurro**	= blue	azzurro	*(mahk-kee-nah) (ah-zoor-rah)* **La macchina è azzurra.** car
(gree-joh) **grigio**	= gray	______	*(leh-leh-fahn-teh)* **L'elefante è grigio.**
(mahr-roh-neh) **marrone**	= brown	______	*(seh-dee-ah)* **La sedia è marrone.** chair
(vehr-deh) **verde**	= green	______	*(lehr-bah)* **L'erba è verde.** grass
(roh-sah) **rosa**	= pink	______	*(fee-oh-reh)* **Il fiore è rosa.** flower
(mool-tee-koh-loh-reh) **multicolore**	= multi-colored	______	*(lahm-pah-dah)* **La lampada è multicolore.**

Now peel off the next *(dee-eh-chee)* **dieci** labels **e** proceed to label these *(koh-loh-ree)* **colori** in your *(kah-sah)* **casa.**

Now let's practice using these **parole.**

Dov'è la barca *(bee-ahn-kah)* **bianca?**	*(ehk-koh)* **Ecco la barca** bianca. there is
Dov'è il tavolo *(gree-joh)* **grigio?**	**Ecco il tavolo** ______.
Dov'è la sedia *(mahr-roh-neh)* **marrone?**	**Ecco la sedia** ______.
Dov'è la palla *(bee-ahn-kah)* **bianca?**	**Ecco la palla** ______.
Dov'è la lampada multicolore?	**Ecco la lampada** ______.
Dov'è il libro *(rohs-soh)* **rosso?**	**Ecco il libro** ______.

- ☐ **dicembre** *(dee-chem-breh)* .... December ______
- ☐ **diretto** *(dee-reht-toh)* .... direct ______
- ☐ **il disastro** *(dee-sah-stroh)* .... disaster, accident ______
- ☐ **la distanza** *(dee-stahn-tsah)* .... distance ______
- ☐ **divino** *(dee-vee-noh)* .... divine ______

Dov'è la porta *(vehr-deh)* verde? Ecco la porta ____________.

Dov'è la casa *(roh-sah)* rosa? Ecco la casa ____________.

Dov'è la banana *(jahl-lah)* gialla? Ecco la banana ____________.

Note: **In** *(een)* **italiano,** *(ee-tah-lee-ah-noh)* the **verbo** *(vehr-boh)* (verb) for "to have" **è "avere,"** *(ah-veh-reh)* which looks like...

ho *(oh)* = I have ____________ **abbiamo** *(ahb-bee-ah-moh)* = we have ____________

Let's review **"vorrei"** *(vohr-reh-ee)* (would like) e learn **"ho"** *(oh)* (I have) and **"abbiamo."** *(ahb-bee-ah-moh)* (we have) **Ripeta** *(ree-peh-tah)* each sentence out loud.

Vorrei un bicchiere di birra. *(vohr-reh-ee)(oon) (beek-kee-eh-reh) (dee)(beer-rah)* (bicchiere = glass)

Vorremmo due bicchieri di vino. *(vohr-rehm-moh) ... (vee-noh)*

Vorrei un bicchiere di acqua. *(ahk-kwah)*

Vorremmo un'insalata. *(oo-neen-sah-lah-tah)*

Vorremmo avere una macchina. *(ah-veh-reh) (mahk-kee-nah)*

Vorremmo avere una macchina in Europa. *(eh-oo-roh-pah)*

Ho un bicchiere di birra. *(oh)*

Abbiamo due bicchieri di vino. *(ahb-bee-ah-moh)*

Abbiamo una casa. *(oo-nah)*

Ho una casa in America. *(een) (ah-meh-ree-kah)*

Ho una macchina. *(mahk-kee-nah)*

Abbiamo una macchina in Europa.

Now fill in the following blanks **con** the **forma** *(fohr-mah)* (form) **corretta** *(kohr-ret-tah)* (correct) of **"avere" o** *(oh)* (or) **"vorrei."** *(voh-reh-ee)*

abbiamo ____________ **tre macchine.**
(we have)

____________ **due biglietti dell'autobus.**
(we would like)

____________ **un quadro.**
(I have)

____________ **sette cartoline.**
(I would like)

- ☐ **il dizionario** *(dee-tsee-oh-nah-ree-oh)* ...... dictionary ____________
- ☐ **il dollaro** *(dohl-lah-roh)* .... dollar ____________
- ☐ **il dottore** *(doht-toh-reh)* .... doctor ____________
- ☐ **il dubbio** *(doob-bee-oh)* .... doubt ____________
- ☐ **durante** *(doo-rahn-teh)* .... during ____________

Ecco a quick review of the **colori** *(koh-loh-ree)*. Draw lines between **le** *(leh)* **parole italiane** *(pah-roh-leh)* **e** *(eh)* and **i** *(ee)* the **colori corretti** *(kohr-ret-tee)*.

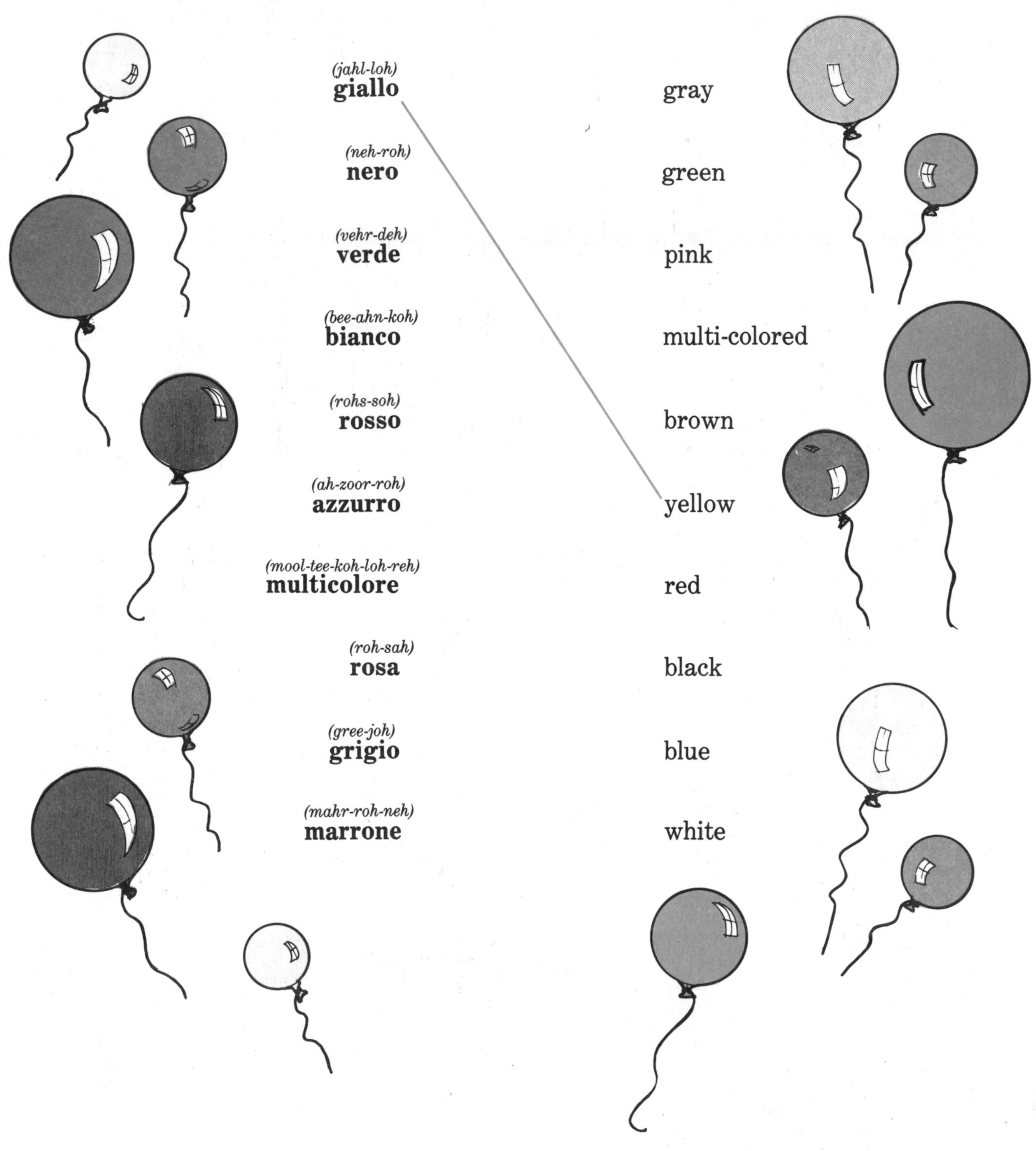

giallo *(jahl-loh)*	gray
nero *(neh-roh)*	green
verde *(vehr-deh)*	pink
bianco *(bee-ahn-koh)*	multi-colored
rosso *(rohs-soh)*	brown
azzurro *(ah-zoor-roh)*	yellow
multicolore *(mool-tee-koh-loh-reh)*	red
rosa *(roh-sah)*	black
grigio *(gree-joh)*	blue
marrone *(mahr-roh-neh)*	white

- ☐ **eccellente** *(eh-chehl-len-teh)*............ excellent ______________
- ☐ **l'economia** *(leh-koh-noh-mee-ah)* .... economy ______________
- ☐ **l'entrata** *(len-trah-tah)*................ entrance ______________
- ☐ **est** *(ehst)*............................ east ______________
- ☐ **Europa** *(eh-oo-roh-pah)* .... Europe ______________

(eel) (deh-nah-roh) Il Denaro
money

Step 6

Before starting this Step, go back **e** review Step 4. Make sure you can count to (ven-tee) **venti** without looking back at **il** (lee-broh) **libro.** Let's learn the larger (noo-meh-ree) **numeri** now, as you will hardly find anything that costs less than 20 (lee-reh) **lire.** After practicing aloud **i numeri italiani** 10 (ah) **a** (to) 100 below, write these **numeri** in the blanks provided. Again, notice the (see-mee-lee-too-dee-nee) **similitudini** between **numeri** such as (kwaht-troh) **quattro** (4), (kwaht-tohr-dee-chee) **quattordici** (14) and (kwah-rahn-tah) **quaranta** (40).

10	(dee-eh-chee) **dieci**	**(quattro + sei = dieci)**	10 dieci, dieci, dieci
20	(ven-tee) **venti**	**(due = 2)**	20 ________
30	(tren-tah) **trenta**	**(tre = 3)**	30 ________
40	(kwah-rahn-tah) **quaranta**	**(quattro = 4)**	40 ________
50	(cheen-kwahn-tah) **cinquanta**	**(cinque = 5)**	50 ________
60	(sehs-sahn-tah) **sessanta**	**(sei = 6)**	60 ________
70	(set-tahn-tah) **settanta**	**(sette = 7)**	70 ________
80	(oht-tahn-tah) **ottanta**	**(otto = 8)**	80 ________
90	(noh-vahn-tah) **novanta**	**(nove = 9)**	90 ________
100	(chen-toh) **cento**		100 ________
1000	(meel-leh) **mille**		1000 ________
2000	(doo-eh) (mee-lah) **due mila**		2000 ________

Now take a logical guess. (koh-meh) **Come** would you write (**e** say) the following? **Le** (ree-spoh-steh) **risposte** (soh-noh) **sono** (are) at the bottom of (lah) **la** (pah-jee-nah) **pagina.**

400 ________ 600 ________

2000 ________ 5300 ________

RISPOSTE

400 = quattrocento
2000 = due mila
600 = seicento
5300 = cinque mila trecento

The unit of currency **in Italia è la** *(lee-rah)* **lira** *(ee-tah-lee-ah-nah)* **italiana,** abbreviated **£.** Bills are called *(beel-yet-tee)* **biglietti** and coins are called *(moh-neh-teh)* **monete.** The **lira** is the only monetary unit **in Italia** and can not be broken down into smaller units. You will find that hundreds of *(lee-reh)* **lire** are equivalent to an American *(dohl-lah-roh)* **dollaro,** so you will want to become very familiar with large numbers. Always be sure to practice each **parola** out loud. You might want to exchange some money *(ah-dehs-soh)* **adesso** (now) so that you can familiarize yourself **con** the various types of *(deh-nah-roh)* **denaro** (money).

Biglietti

(cheen-kweh-chen-toh)
cinquecento lire
500

(meel-leh)
mille lire
1,000

(doo-eh) *(mee-lah)*
due mila lire
2,000

(cheen-kweh)
cinque mila lire
5,000

(dee-eh-chee)
dieci mila lire
10,000

(ven-tee)
venti mila lire
20,000

(cheen-kwahn-tah)
cinquanta mila lire
50,000

(chen-toh)
cento mila lire
100,000

Monete

(dee-eh-chee)
dieci lire
10

(ven-tee)
venti lire
20

(cheen-kwahn-tah)
cinquanta lire
50

(chen-toh)
cento lire
100

(doo-eh) *(chen-toh)*
due cento lire
200

(cheen-kweh-chen-toh)
cinquecento lire
500

- ☐ **la famiglia** *(fah-meel-yah)* .... family
- ☐ **famoso** *(fah-moh-soh)* .... famous
- ☐ **la farmacia** *(fahr-mah-chee-ah)* .... pharmacy, drugstore
- ☐ **il favore** *(fah-voh-reh)* .... favor
  - **—per favore** *(pehr) (fah-voh-reh)* .... please

Review **i numeri dieci** through **mille** again. *(ah-dehs-soh)* **Adesso,** (now) how do you say "twenty-two" *(oh)* **o** (or) "fifty-three" *(een)* **in italiano?** You basically put **i numeri** together in a logical sequence: for example, 62 (60 + 2) is **sessantadue** (60 2). See if you can say **e** write **i numeri** on this **pagina. Le risposte** *(soh-noh)* **sono** at the bottom of **la pagina.**

a. 25 =	______ (20 + 5)	e. 36 =	______ (30 + 6)
b. 47 =	______ (40 + 7)	f. 93 =	______ (90 + 3)
c. 84 =	______ (80 + 4)	g. 68 =	sessantotto (60 + 8)
d. 51 =	______ (50 + 1)	h. 72 =	______ (70 + 2)

To ask what something costs **in italiano,** one asks, *(kwahn-toh) (koh-stah)* "**Quanto costa?**"

(ah-dehs-soh) **Adesso** answer the following questions based on **i numeri** in parentheses.

1. *(kwahn-toh) (koh-stah)* **Quanto costa?** — *(koh-stah)* **Costa** dieci (10) *(lee-reh)* **lire.**
2. **Quanto costa?** — **Costa** ______ (20) **lire.**
3. **Quanto costa il** *(lee-broh)* **libro?** — **Costa** ______ (17) **lire.**
4. **Quanto costa** *(lah-oo-toh)* **l'auto?** — **Costa** ______ (90,000) **lire.**
5. **Quanto costa il** *(feelm)* **film?** — **Costa** ______ (3,000) **lire.**
6. **Quanto costa la** *(kah-meh-rah)* **camera** (room)**?** — **Costa** ______ (15,000) **lire.**
7. **Quanto costa il** *(kwah-droh)* **quadro?** — **Costa** ______ (100,000) **lire.**

RISPOSTE

a. **venticinque**
b. **quarantasette**
c. **ottantaquattro**
d. **cinquantuno**
e. **trentasei**
f. **novantatré**
g. **sessantotto**
h. **settantadue**

1. **dieci**
2. **venti**
3. **diciassette**
4. **novanta mila**
5. **tre mila**
6. **quindici mila**
7. **cento mila**

Step 7

(oh-jee) **Oggi,** *(doh-mah-nee)* **Domani, e** *(ee-eh-ree)* **Ieri**

today, tomorrow, yesterday

(kah-len-dah-ree-oh) Il calendario
calendar

(set-tee-mah-nah) *(ah)* *(johr-nee)*
Una settimana ha sette giorni.
week has days

(loo-neh-dee) lunedì	*(mahr-teh-dee)* martedì	*(mehr-koh-leh-dee)* mercoledì	*(joh-veh-dee)* giovedì	*(veh-nehr-dee)* venerdì	*(sah-bah-toh)* sabato	*(doh-meh-nee-kah)* domenica
1	2	3	4	5	6	7

(mohl-toh) *(eem-pohr-tahn-teh)*
È molto importante to know the days of the week **e** the various parts of the day.
it is very important

Let's learn them. Be sure to say them aloud before filling in the blanks below.

(l-yee)(ee-tah-lee-ah-nee) *(set-tee-mah-nah)* *(loo-neh-dee)*
Gli Italiani begin counting their **settimana** on Monday with **lunedì.**
the Italians week

(loo-neh-dee) **lunedì** lunedì ____________
Monday

(mahr-teh-dee) **martedì** ____________
Tuesday

(mehr-koh-leh-dee) **mercoledì** ____________
Wednesday

(joh-veh-dee) **giovedì** ____________
Thursday

(veh-nehr-dee) **venerdì** ____________
Friday

(sah-bah-toh) **sabato** ____________
Saturday

(doh-meh-nee-kah) **domenica** ____________
Sunday

If *(oh-jee)* **oggi** (today) **è mercoledì,** then *(doh-mah-nee)* **domani** (tomorrow) **è giovedì e** *(ee-eh-ree)* **ieri** (yesterday) *(eh-rah)* **era** (was) **martedì. Adesso,** you supply **le risposte corrette.** If **oggi è lunedì,** then **domani è** ____________ **e ieri era** ____________. **O,** if **oggi è lunedì,** then ____________ **è martedì e** ieri ____________ **era domenica.** *(keh)* **Che** (what) *(johr-noh)* **giorno** (day) **è** (is) **oggi? Oggi è** ____________.

(ah-dehs-soh) **Adesso,** peel off the next *(set-teh)* **sette** labels **e** put them on a *(kah-len-dah-ree-oh)* **calendario** you use every day.

From *(oh-jee)* **oggi** on, Monday **è "lunedì."**

- ☐ **il filtro** *(feel-troh)* .... filter ____________
- ☐ **finalmente** *(fee-nahl-mehn-teh)* .... finally ____________
- ☐ **finito** *(fee-nee-toh)* .... finished, ended ____________
- ☐ **la fontana** *(fohn-tah-nah)* .... fountain ____________
- ☐ **la forchetta** *(fohr-keht-tah)* .... fork ____________

There are *(kwaht-troh)* **quattro** parts to each *(johr-noh)* **giorno** (day).

morning = *(maht-tee-nah)* **mattina**	
afternoon = *(poh-meh-ree-joh)* **pomeriggio**	
evening = *(seh-rah)* **sera**	sera, sera, sera, sera, sera
night = *(noht-teh)* **notte**	

Notice that the Italian days of the *(set-tee-mah-nah)* **settimana** (week) are not capitalized as **in inglese.** *(ah-dehs-soh)* **Adesso,** fill in the following blanks **e** then check your **risposte** at the bottom of **la pagina.**

a.	Sunday morning	=	domenica mattina
b.	Friday evening	=	
c.	Saturday evening	=	
d.	Monday morning	=	
e.	Wednesday morning	=	
f.	Tuesday afternoon	=	
g.	Thursday afternoon	=	
h.	Thursday evening	=	
i.	yesterday evening	=	
j.	yesterday morning	=	
k.	tomorrow evening	=	
l.	tomorrow afternoon	=	
m.	yesterday afternoon	=	

RISPOSTE

a. **domenica mattina**
b. **venerdì sera**
c. **sabato sera**
d. **lunedì mattina**
e. **mercoledì mattina**
f. **martedì pomeriggio**
g. **giovedì pomeriggio**
h. **giovedì sera**
i. **ieri sera**
j. **ieri mattina**
k. **domani sera**
l. **domani pomeriggio**
m. **ieri pomeriggio**

So, **con** *(kohn)* merely **undici** *(oon-dee-chee)* **parole,** you can specify any day of the **settimana** *(set-tee-mah-nah)* **e** any time of the **giorno.** *(johr-noh)* **Le parole "oggi,"** *(oh-jee)* **"domani" e "ieri"** *(ee-eh-ree)* will be **molto** *(mohl-toh)* very **importanti** *(eem-pohr-tahn-tee)* for you in making **prenotazioni** *(preh-noh-tah-tsee-oh-nee)* reservations **e appuntamenti,** *(ahp-poon-tah-men-tee)* appointments in getting **biglietti teatrali** *(beel-yet-tee) (teh-ah-trah-lee)* theater tickets **e** many things you will want to do. Knowing the parts of **il giorno** will help you to learn **e** understand the various **saluti** *(sah-loo-tee)* greetings **italiani** *(ee-tah-lee-ah-nee)* below. Practice these every day now until your trip.

good morning / good afternoon	=	*(bwohn) (johr-noh)* **buon giorno**	________
good evening	=	*(bwoh-nah) (seh-rah)* **buona sera**	________
good night	=	*(bwoh-nah)(noht-teh)* **buona notte**	buona notte
hi!/bye!	=	*(chah-oh)* **ciao**	________
How are you?	=	*(koh-meh) (vah)* **Come va?**	________

Take the next **quattro** labels **e** stick them on the appropriate **cose** *(koh-seh)* things in your **casa.** *(kah-sah)* How about the bathroom mirror **per** *(pehr)* for **"buon giorno"?** **O** the front door **per "buona sera"?** **O** your alarm clock **per "buona notte"?** Remember that, whenever you enter small shops **e** stores **in Italia,** you will hear the appropriate **saluto** *(sah-loo-toh)* greeting for the time of day. Don't be surprised. It is a **molto** *(mohl-toh)* very friendly **e** warm **costume.** *(koh-stoo-meh)* custom Everyone greets everyone **e** you should too, if you really want to enjoy **l'Italia.** You **è** about one-fourth of your way through **il libro** *(lee-broh)* **ed è** *(ed) (eh)* a good time to quickly review **le parole** you have learned before doing the crossword puzzle on the next **pagina. Buon divertimento** *(bwohn) (dee-vehr-tee-men-toh)* have fun **e buona** *(bwoh-nah)* good **fortuna.** *(for-too-nah)* luck

RISPOSTE TO CROSSWORD PUZZLE (PAROLE CROCIATE)

ACROSS

1. vorrei
2. parete
3. grigio
4. signore
5. luce
6. pittura
7. domenica
8. con
9. moneta
10. cinque
11. denaro
12. nero
13. giallo
14. chi
15. giorno
16. risposta
17. avere
18. orologio
19. tre
21. quanto
22. multicolore
23. sera
24. oggi
25. perché
26. notte
27. ecco
28. abbiamo

DOWN

1. venerdì
2. ieri
3. angolo
4. sedia
5. sabato
6. diciannove
7. pomeriggio
8. acqua
9. banca
10. cartolina
11. donna
13. ciao
14. che è
15. soffitto
16. verde
17. bianco
19. tendina
20. lampada
21. quattro
22. martedì
23. due
24. rosso
25. come

CROSSWORD PUZZLE (PAROLE CROCIATE)
(kroh-chah-teh)

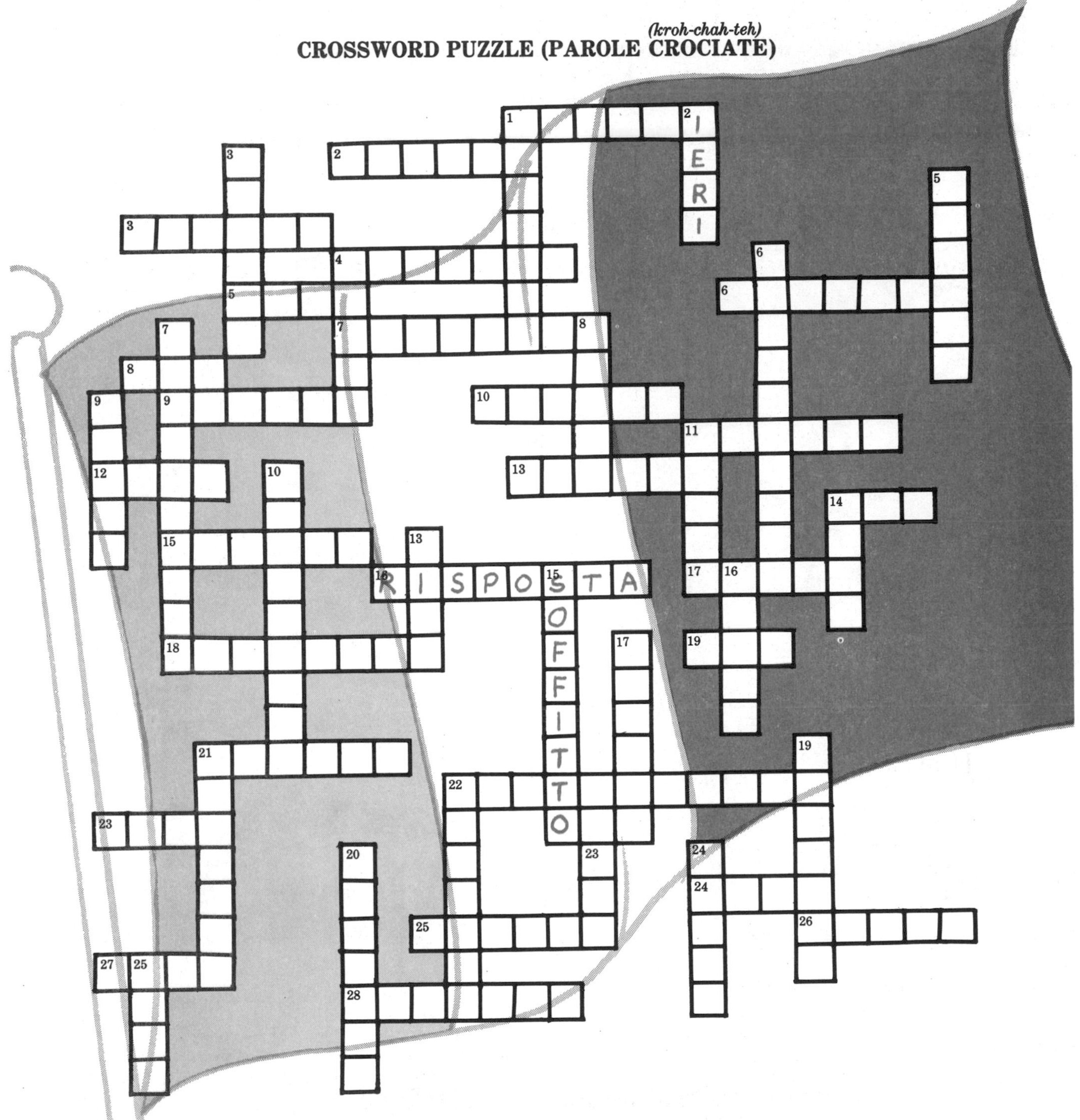

ACROSS

1. I would like
2. wall
3. gray
4. gentleman
5. light
6. paint
7. Sunday
8. with
9. coin
10. five
11. money
12. black
13. yellow
14. who
15. day
16. answer
17. to have
18. clock
19. three
21. how much
22. multi-colored
23. evening
24. today
25. why
26. night
27. there is/are
28. we have

DOWN

1. Friday
2. yesterday
3. corner
4. chair
5. Saturday
6. nineteen
7. afternoon
8. water
9. bank
10. postcard
11. woman
13. hi!/bye!
14. what is
15. ceiling
16. green
17. white
19. curtain
20. lamp
21. four
22. Tuesday
23. two
24. red
25. how

Step 8

In, Sopra, Sotto . . .
(een) (soh-prah) (soht-toh)
in, over, under

Le preposizioni italiane *(preh-poh-see-tsee-oh-nee)* (words like "in," "on," "through" and "next to") **sono** (are) very useful **e** they allow you to be precise **con** a minimum of effort. Instead of having to point **sei** *(seh-ee)* times at a piece of yummy pastry you wish to order, you can explain precisely which one you want by saying **è** *(eh)* (it is) behind, in front of, next to, **o** under the piece of the pastry the salesperson is starting to pick up. Let's learn some of these **piccole** *(peek-koh-leh)* (little) **parole** which **sono molto** *(mohl-toh)* **simili** *(see-mee-lee)* (similar) to **inglese.** Study the **esempi** *(eh-sem-pee)* (examples) below.

da *(dah)* (often seen as **dal, dalla,** *(dahl) (dahl-lah)* (from the) etc.) = of/from
in *(een)* (often seen as **nel, nella, etc.)** *(nel) (nel-lah)* = into/in
accanto a *(ahk-kahn-toh) (ah)* = next to
sotto *(soht-toh)* = under
sopra *(soh-prah)* = over

Il signore entra nel nuovo albergo.
(ehn-trah) (nel) (noo-oh-voh) (ahl-behr-goh)
enters, in the, new, hotel

La donna viene dall'eccellente albergo.
(dohn-nah) (vee-eh-neh) (dahl) (eh-chel-len-teh)
woman, comes, from the excellent

Il medico è nel buon albergo.
(meh-dee-koh) (bwohn)
physician, good

Il nuovo quadro è sopra il tavolo.
(soh-prah) (tah-voh-loh)
table

Il nuovo quadro è accanto all'orologio.
(ahk-kahn-toh) (oh-roh-loh-joh)
clock

Il cane grigio è sotto il tavolo marrone.
(kah-neh) (soht-toh)
dog

Il tavolo marrone è sopra il cane.

L'orologio verde è sopra il tavolo.

L'orologio verde è accanto al quadro.

☐ **la foresta** *(foh-reh-stah)* . . . . forest ______
☐ **la forma** *(fohr-mah)* . . . . form ______
☐ **Francia** *(frahn-chah)* . . . . France ______
☐ **fresco** *(freh-skoh)* . . . . cool, fresh ______
☐ **la frutta** *(froot-tah)* . . . . fruit ______

Fill in the blanks below **con le** *(preh-poh-see-tsee-oh-nee)* **preposizioni corrette** according to the *(eel-loo-strah-tsee-oh-nee)* **illustrazioni** (pictures) on the previous **pagina.**

Il signore entra __________ nuovo *(ahl-behr-goh)* **albergo.**

Il cane grigio è sotto **il tavolo.**

(loh-roh-loh-joh) **L'orologio verde è __________ il** *(tah-voh-loh)* **tavolo.**

Il medico è __________ buon albergo.

L'orologio verde è __________ al quadro.

Il nuovo quadro è __________ il tavolo.

Il tavolo marrone è __________ il quadro.

Il nuovo quadro è __________ all'orologio.

La donna viene __________ *(eh-chel-len-teh)* **eccellente albergo.**

Il tavolo marrone è __________ l'orologio.

(ah-dehs-soh) **Adesso, risponda alle** (to the) *(doh-mahn-deh)* **domande** (questions) based on **le** *(eel-loo-strah-tsee-oh-nee)* **illustrazioni** on the previous **pagina.**

(doh-veh) *(eel)* **Dov'è il medico?** ______________________________

Dov'è il *(kah-neh)* **cane?** ______________________________

Dov'è il tavolo? ______________________________

Dov'è il quadro? ______________________________

(keh) *(fah)* **Che fa** (does) **la donna?** ______________________________

(keh) *(fah)* **Che fa** (does) **il signore?** ______________________________

È (is) **verde l'orologio?** Sí, l'orologio è verde.

È (is) **grigio il cane?** Sí, ______________________________

- ☐ **la galleria** *(gahl-leh-ree-ah)* .... gallery __________
- ☐ **gennaio** *(jehn-nah-ee-oh)* .... January __________
- ☐ **gentile** *(jehn-tee-leh)* .... gentle, kind __________
- ☐ **la geografia** *(jeh-oh-grah-fee-ah)* .... geography __________
- ☐ **la giacca** *(jahk-kah)* .... jacket __________

Adesso for some more practice **con le preposizioni italiane.**

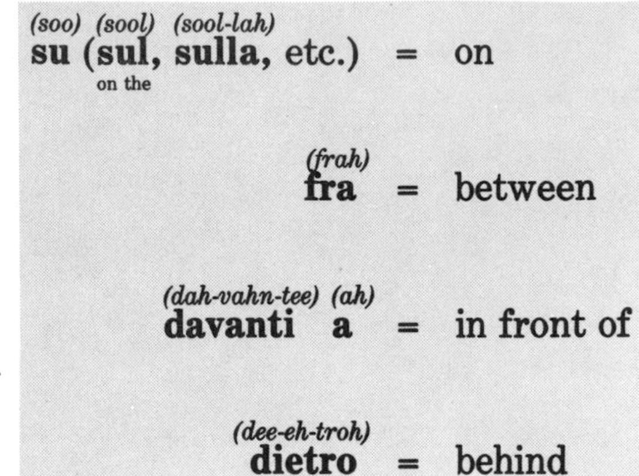

(soo) (sool) (sool-lah) **su (sul, sulla, etc.)** (sul = on the)	=	on
(frah) **fra**	=	between
(dah-vahn-tee) (ah) **davanti a**	=	in front of
(dee-eh-troh) **dietro**	=	behind

Il bicchiere (beek-kee-eh-reh) **di** (dee) (of) **acqua** (ahk-kwah) **è sul** (sool) (on the) **tavolo.**	**Il bicchiere di acqua è __________ tavolo.**
Il letto è dietro (dee-eh-troh) **il tavolo.**	**Il letto è __dietro__ il tavolo.**
La lampada gialla è dietro il tavolo.	**La lampada gialla è __________ il tavolo.**
Il tavolo marrone è davanti (dah-vahn-tee) **al** (ahl) (of the) **letto.**	**Il tavolo è _______________ letto.**
La lampada gialla è fra (frah) **il tavolo e il letto.**	**La lampada gialla è __________ il tavolo e il letto.**

Risponda alle (ahl-leh) (to the) **domande,** based on **le illustrazioni,** by filling in the blanks **con le preposizioni corrette.** Choose **le preposizioni** from those you have just learned.

Dov'è il libro rosso?

Il libro rosso è __________ tavolo marrone.

Dov'è l'autobus azzurro?

L'autobus azzurro è ______ all'albergo grigio.

- ☐ **il giardino** *(jahr-dee-noh)* .... garden __________
- ☐ **giugno** *(joon-yoh)* .... June __________
- ☐ **il governo** *(goh-vehr-noh)* .... government __________
- ☐ **grande** *(grahn-deh)* .... grand, big, large __________
- ☐ **la guida** *(gwee-dah)* .... guide __________

Dov'è la finestra? (fee-neh-strah) window **Dov'è il tappeto verde?** (tahp-peh-toh) carpet **Dov'è il vaso?** (vah-soh) vase

Il quadro è ______________________ **alla finestra.**

Il vaso è ______________________ **tavolo nero.**

Il quadro è sopra **il tavolo nero.**

Il tappeto verde è ______________________ **il tavolo nero.**

Il tavolo nero è ______________________ **il quadro.**

Adesso, fill in each blank on **il palazzo** (pah-lah-tsoh) palace below **con** the best possible **preposizione.**

Le risposte corrette sono at the bottom of **la pagina. Buon divertimento.** have fun

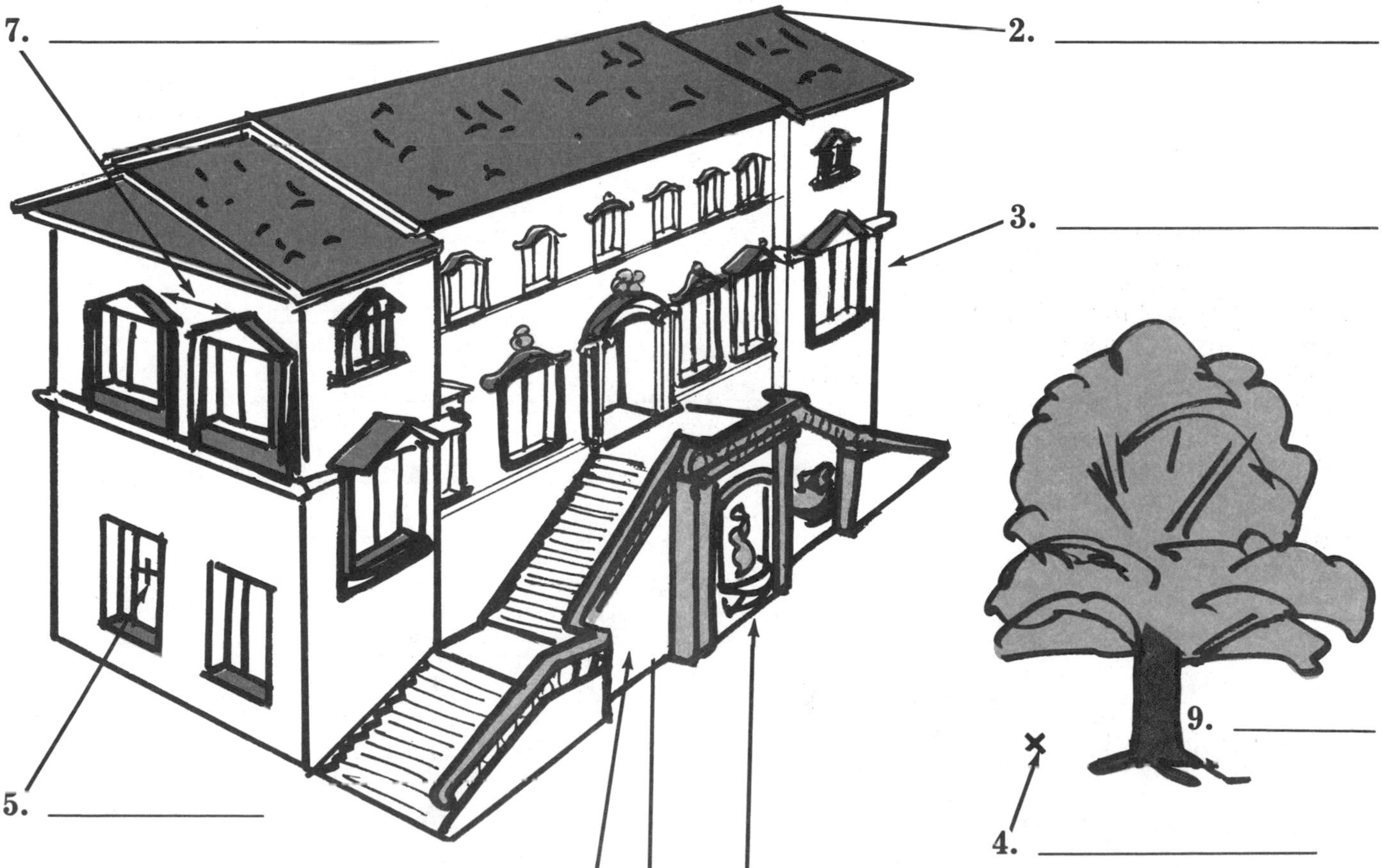

1. ______________________
2. ______________________
3. ______________________
4. ______________________
5. ______________________
6. ______________________
7. ______________________
8. davanti a
9. ______________________
10. ______________________

RISPOSTE

1. **sopra**	3. **dietro**	5. **in**	7. **accanto a**	9. **sotto**
2. **su**	4. **fra**	6. **in**	8. **davanti a**	10. **da**

Step 9

(jehn-nah-ee-oh) Gennaio, (fehb-brah-ee-oh) Febbraio, (mar-tsoh) Marzo
January, February, March

Trenta giorni (ah) ha (has) (set-tem-breh) settembre, (ah-pree-leh) aprile, (joon-yoh) giugno e (noh-vem-breh) novembre . . .

Sound familiar? You have learned the days of **la (set-tee-mah-nah) settimana,** so **adesso è (it is) il (the) (moh-men-toh) momento (moment)** to learn **i (meh-see) mesi (months) dell' (of the) (ahn-noh) anno (year) e** the different kinds of **(tem-poh) tempo (weather)** you might encounter on your holiday. For **(eh-sem-pee-oh) esempio (example),** you ask about **il (tem-poh) tempo in italiano** just as you would **in inglese:** **"(keh) Che tempo (fah) fa (does it make) oggi (today)?"** Practice all the possible answers to this **(doh-mahn-dah) domanda e (poh-ee) poi (then)** write **le risposte** in the blanks below.

(keh) Che (tem-poh) tempo (weather) (fah) fa (oh-jee) oggi?

(pee-oh-veh) Piove (it rains) oggi. ______________________________

(neh-vee-kah) Nevica (it snows) oggi. ______________________________

(fah) Fa (freh-skoh) fresco (cool) oggi. ______________________________

Fa (frehd-doh) freddo (cold) oggi. ______________________________

Fa bel (nice) (tem-poh) tempo oggi. ______________________________

Fa (kaht-tee-voh) cattivo (bad) tempo oggi. *Fa cattivo tempo oggi.*

Fa (kahl-doh) caldo (warm/hot) oggi. ______________________________

(cheh) C'è (nehb-bee-ah) nebbia (fog) oggi. ______________________________

Adesso, practice **le parole** on the next **pagina** aloud **e (poh-ee) poi (then)** fill in the blanks with **i (noh-mee) nomi** of **i (meh-see) mesi (months) e** the appropriate weather report. Notice that, **in italiano,** the months of the year and the days of the week are not capitalized.

- ☐ **incantevole** *(een-kahn-teh-voh-leh)* .... enchanting, charming ______________
- ☐ **indispensabile** *(een-dee-spen-sah-bee-leh)*... indispensable ______________
- ☐ **l'individuo** *(leen-dee-vee-doo-oh)* .... individual (person) ______________
- ☐ **l'industria** *(leen-doo-stree-ah)* .... industry ______________
- ☐ **industrioso** *(een-doo-stree-oh-soh)*......... industrious ______________

(een) (jehn-nah-ee-oh)
in gennaio ______ | (neh-vee-kah) **Nevica in gennaio.** ______

(fehb-brah-ee-oh)
in febbraio ______ | (ahn-keh) **Nevica anche in febbraio.** ______ (anche = also)

(mar-tsoh)
in marzo in marzo | (pee-oh-veh) **Piove in marzo.** ______

(ah-pree-leh)
in aprile ______ | **Piove anche in aprile.** ______

(mah-joh)
in maggio ______ | (tee-rah) (vehn-toh) **Tira vento in maggio.** ______ (it's windy)

(joon-yoh)
in giugno ______ | (cheh) (soh-leh) **C'è sole in giugno.** C'è sole in giugno. (there is sun)

(lool-yoh)
in luglio ______ | (tem-poh) **Fa bel tempo in luglio.** ______

(ah-goh-stoh)
in agosto ______ | (kahl-doh) **Fa caldo in agosto.** ______

(set-tem-breh)
in settembre ______ | (nehb-bee-ah) **C'è nebbia in settembre.** ______ (fog)

(oht-toh-breh)
in ottobre ______ | (freh-skoh) **Fa fresco in ottobre.** ______

(noh-vem-breh)
in novembre ______ | (kaht-tee-voh) **Fa cattivo tempo in novembre.** ______

(dee-chem-breh)
in dicembre ______ | (frehd-doh) **Fa freddo in dicembre.** ______

Adesso, risponda alle domande based on **le illustrazioni** to the right.

Che tempo fa in febbraio? ______

Che tempo fa in aprile? ______

Che tempo fa in maggio? ______

Che tempo fa in agosto? Fa ______

Che tempo fa oggi, bello o cattivo? ______

- ☐ **l'influenza** *(leen-floo-en-tsah)* . . . . influence ______
- ☐ **l'informazione** *(leen-fohr-mah-tsee-oh-neh)* . . . information ______
- ☐ **l'ingegnere** *(leen-jehn-yeh-reh)* . . . . engineer ______
- ☐ **l'Inghilterra** *(leen-gheel-tehr-rah)* . . . . England ______
- ☐ **innamorato** *(een-nah-moh-rah-toh)* . . . . enamored ______

Adesso, le stagioni dell'anno . . .
(stah-joh-nee) seasons *(ahn-noh)*

(leen-vehr-noh) **l'inverno** winter	*(leh-stah-teh)* **l'estate** summer	*(lah-oo-toon-noh)* **l'autunno** autumn	*(pree-mah-veh-rah)* **la primavera** spring

______	l'estate	______	______
Fa freddo *(een) (een-vehr-noh)* **in inverno.**	**Fa caldo** *(een) (eh-stah-teh)* **in estate.**	*(tee-rah)* **Tira vento** it's *(ah-oo-toon-noh)* **in autunno.**	**Piove in** *(pree-mah-veh-rah)* **primavera.**

At this point, **è** *(eh)* **una** *(oo-nah)* **buona** *(bwoh-nah)* good **idea** *(ee-deh-ah)* idea to familiarize yourself **con le temperature** *(tem-peh-rah-too-reh)* temperatures **europee.** *(eh-oo-roh-peh)* European Carefully read the typical weather forecasts below **e** study **il termometro,** *(tehr-moh-meh-troh)* thermometer because **le temperature in Europa** *(eh-oo-roh-pah)* are calculated on the basis of Centigrade (not Fahrenheit).

Fahrenheit		**Celsius**	
212° F	——	100° C	*(ahk-kwah) (bohl-leh)* **l'acqua bolle** boils
98.6° F	——	37° C	**temperatura normale del sangue** *(sahn-goo-eh)* of blood
68° F	——	20° C	
32° F	——	0° C	**l'acqua dolce gela** *(dohl-cheh) (jeh-lah)* water fresh freezes
0° F	——	-17.8° C	**l'acqua salata gela** *(sah-lah-tah)* water salt freezes
-10° F	——	-23.3° C	

Il tempo per lunedì 21 marzo:

freddo con vento
(tehm-peh-rah-too-rah) **temperatura:** **5 gradi** *(grah-dee)* degrees

Il tempo per martedì 18 luglio:

bello e caldo
nice
temperatura: 20 gradi

- ☐ **l'insalata** *(leen-sah-lah-tah)* . . . . salad
- ☐ **interamente** *(een-teh-rah-men-teh)* . . . . entirely
- ☐ **interessante** *(een-teh-rehs-sahn-teh)* . . . . interesting
- ☐ **l'invito** *(leen-vee-toh)* . . . . invitation
- ☐ **l'isola** *(lee-soh-lah)* . . . . island

(fah-meel-yah) Famiglia, (fah-meh) fame, e (feh-deh) fede
family, hunger, faith

Just as we have the three "R's" **in inglese, in italiano** there are the three "F's" which help us to understand some of the basics of **la** *(vee-tah)* **vita** (life) *(ee-tah-lee-ah-nah)* **italiana.** (Italian)

Famiglia 

Fame 

Fede 

Study **le illustrazioni** below **e** *(poh-ee)* **poi** (then) write out **le** *(noo-oh-vee)* **nuove** (new) **parole** in the blanks that follow.

(lah-beh-roh) **L'albero** (tree) *(jeh-neh-ah-loh-jee-koh)* **genealogico** (genealogical)

(pah-oh-loh) (bee-ahn-kee)
Paolo Bianchi
(signor Bianchi)

(klah-oo-dee-ah)
Claudia Bianchi
(signora Bianchi)

(fee-leep-poh) (mahn-freh-dee)
Filippo Manfredi
(signor Manfredi)

(sahn-drah)
Sandra Manfredi
(signora Manfredi)

(nee-koh-lah)
Nicola Bianchi

(mah-ree-ah)
Maria Bianchi

(fah-meel-yah) **la famiglia**
family

(joh-vahn-nee)
Giovanni
(signor Bianchi)

(eh-leh-nah)
Elena
(signorina Bianchi)

- ☐ **il lago** *(lah-goh)* .... lake ____________
- ☐ **largo** *(lahr-goh)* .... wide, broad ____________
- ☐ **il legume** *(leh-goo-meh)* .... vegetable ____________
- ☐ **la lettera** *(let-teh-rah)* .... letter ____________
- ☐ **la lezione** *(leh-tsee-oh-neh)* .... lesson, lecture ____________

(ee)(nohn-nee)
i nonni
grandparents

(jeh-nee-toh-ree)
i genitori
parents

(nohn-noh)
il nonno il nonno
grandfather

(nohn-nah)
la nonna ____________________
grandmother

(pah-dreh)
il padre ____________________
father

(mah-dreh)
la madre ____________________
mother

(feel-yee)
i figli
children

(pah-ren-tee)
i parenti
relatives

(feel-yoh)
il figlio ____________________
son

(feel-yah)
la figlia ____________________
daughter

(zee-oh)
lo zio ____________________
uncle

(zee-ah)
la zia ____________________
aunt

Il figlio e la figlia sono anche (also) **fratello** (frah-tel-loh) (brother) **e sorella** (soh-rel-lah) (sister)**.**

Let's learn how to identify **la famiglia** *(fah-meel-yah)* by **nome** *(noh-meh)*. Study the following **esempi** *(eh-sem-pee)* (examples).

Come (how) **si** *(see)* (is) **chiama** *(kee-ah-mah)* (called) **il padre** (the father)**?**

Il padre si chiama Nicola.

Come si (is) **chiama** *(kee-ah-mah)* (called) **la madre?**

La madre si chiama (is called) Maria.

Adesso you fill in the following blanks, **basato** *(bah-sah-toh)* (based) **sulle** *(sool-leh)* (on the) **illustrazioni,** in the same manner.

Come si chiama il figlio?

________ **si chiama** ________.

Come si chiama ________?

________ **si chiama** ________.

- ☐ **libero** *(lee-beh-roh)* .... free, liberated ________
- ☐ **la lingua** *(leen-goo-ah)* .... language ________
- ☐ **la lista** *(lee-stah)* .... list ________
- ☐ **la lotteria** *(loht-teh-ree-ah)* .... lottery ________
- ☐ **lungo** *(loon-goh)* .... long ________

Study all these **illustrazioni e poi** practice

saying **e** writing out **le parole.**

Ecco la cucina.

(free-goh-ree-feh-roh) **il frigorifero**	*(koo-chee-nah)* **la cucina**	*(vee-noh)* **il vino**
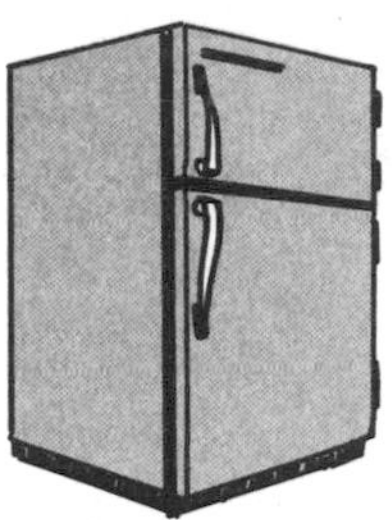		
________________	________________	________________
(beer-rah) **la birra**	*(laht-teh)* **il latte**	*(boor-roh)* **il burro**
		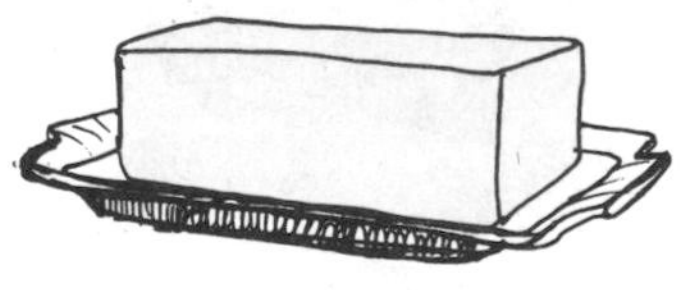
________________	il latte	________________

Risponda alle domande aloud.

Dov'è la birra? .... **La birra è nel** *(free-goh-ree-feh-roh)* **frigorifero.**

Dov'è il latte? **Dov'è il vino?** **Dov'è il burro?**

- ☐ **il maestro** *(mah-eh-stroh)* .... master, teacher ________________
- ☐ **magnifico** *(mahn-yee-fee-koh)* .... magnificent ________________
- ☐ **la maniera** *(mah-nee-eh-rah)*........... manner, way ________________
- ☐ **marzo** *(mahr-tsoh)* .... March ________________
- ☐ **il matrimonio** *(mah-tree-moh-nee-oh)* ... marriage ________________

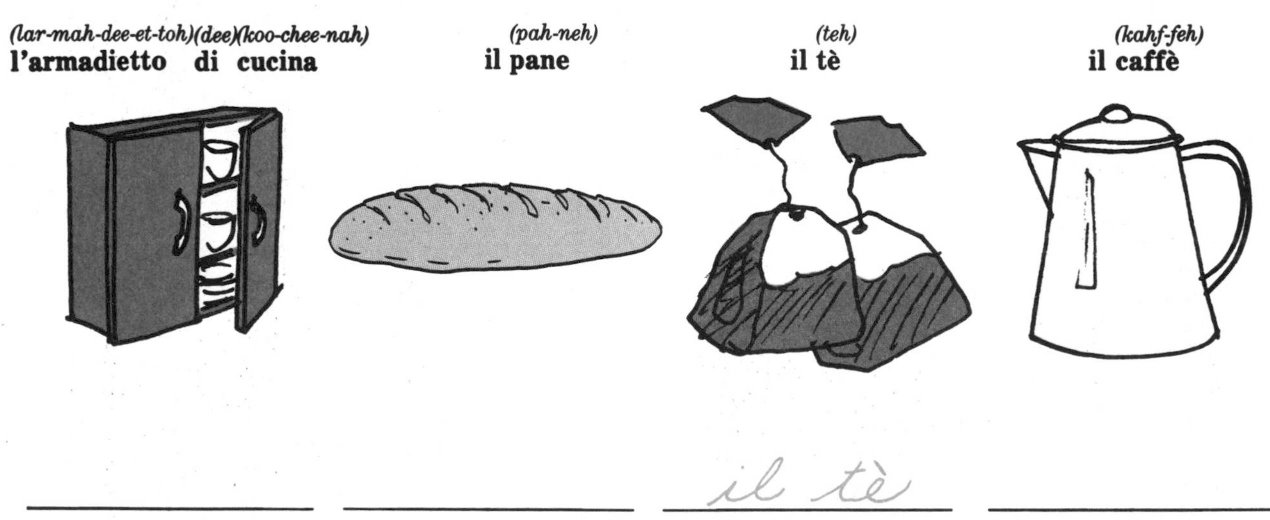

Dov'è il pane? Il pane è nell'armadietto. Dov'è il tè? Dov'è il caffè? Dov'è il sale? Dov'è il pepe? Adesso *(ah-prah)* **apra** (open) your **libro** to the **pagina con** the labels **e** remove the next *(dee-chahn-noh-veh)* **diciannove** labels **e** proceed to label all these **cose** in your **casa.** Do not forget to use every opportunity to say these **parole** out loud. **È molto** *(eem-por-tahn-teh)* **importante!**

- ☐ **il medico** *(meh-dee-koh)* .... medical doctor, physician __________
- ☐ **la memoria** *(meh-moh-ree-ah)*.......... memory __________
- ☐ **meno** *(meh-noh)* .... minus, less __________
- ☐ **meraviglioso** *(meh-rah-veel-yoh-soh)* .... marvelous __________
- ☐ **il mercato** *(mehr-kah-toh)* .... market __________

(kee-eh-sah) La chiesa
church

In Italia, there is not the wide variety of **religioni** *(reh-lee-joh-nee)* religions that **abbiamo** *(ahb-bee-ah-moh)* we have **qui** *(kwee)* here **in America.**

A person's **religione** *(reh-lee-joh-neh)* **è generalmente** *(jeh-neh-rahl-men-teh)* generally one of the following.

1. ***cattolica** *(kaht-toh-lee-kah)* Catholic cattolica
2. **protestante** *(proh-teh-stahn-teh)* Protestant ______
3. **ebraica,** *(eh-brah-ee-kah)* **ebreo** *(eh-breh-oh)* Jewish ______

Ecco una cattedrale *(kaht-teh-drah-leh)* cathedral **in Italia.** →

È una cattedrale cattolica o protestante?

È una nuova cattedrale? No, è una vecchia *(vehk-kee-ah)* old **cattedrale.** You will see **molte** *(mohl-teh)* many **belle** *(bel-leh)* beautiful **cattedrali** *(kaht-teh-drah-lee)* like this during your holiday **in Italia.**

Adesso let's learn how to say "I am" **in italiano:** I am = **io** *(ee-oh)* **sono** *(soh-noh)* ______.

Practice saying **"io sono" con** the following **parole. Adesso** write each sentence for more practice.

Io sono cattolico. ______ **Io sono protestante.** ______

Io sono ebreo. Io sono ebreo. **Io sono americano.** ______

Io sono in Europa *(eh-oo-roh-pah)***.** ______ **Io sono in Italia.** ______

*To make an adjective feminine **in italiano,** you usually change the **o** at the end of the word to an **a.** Adjectives that end in **e** are both masculine and feminine.

- ☐ **il metallo** *(meh-tahl-loh)* .... metal ______
- ☐ **il metro** *(meh-troh)* .... meter ______
- ☐ **milione** *(mee-lee-oh-neh)* .... million ______
- ☐ **la misura** *(mee-soo-rah)* .... measure, size ______
- ☐ **la moda** *(moh-dah)* .... style, fashion, mode ______

Io sono *(nel-lah)* **nella** (in the) *(kee-eh-sah)* **chiesa.** (church) ____________ **Io sono nella** *(koo-chee-nah)* **cucina.** (kitchen) ____________

Io sono la madre. Io sono la madre. **Io sono il padre.** ____________

Io sono nell'albergo. ____________ **Io sono** *(stahn-koh)* **stanco.** (tired) ____________

Adesso identify all **le** *(pehr-soh-neh)* **persone** (people) **nell'illustrazione** below. On the *(lee-neh-eh)* **linee,** (lines) write **le parole corrette in italiano** for each **persona** corresponding to **il numero** *(soht-toh)* **sotto** (under) **l'illustrazione** *(een-dee-vee-doo-ah-leh)* **individuale.** (individual)

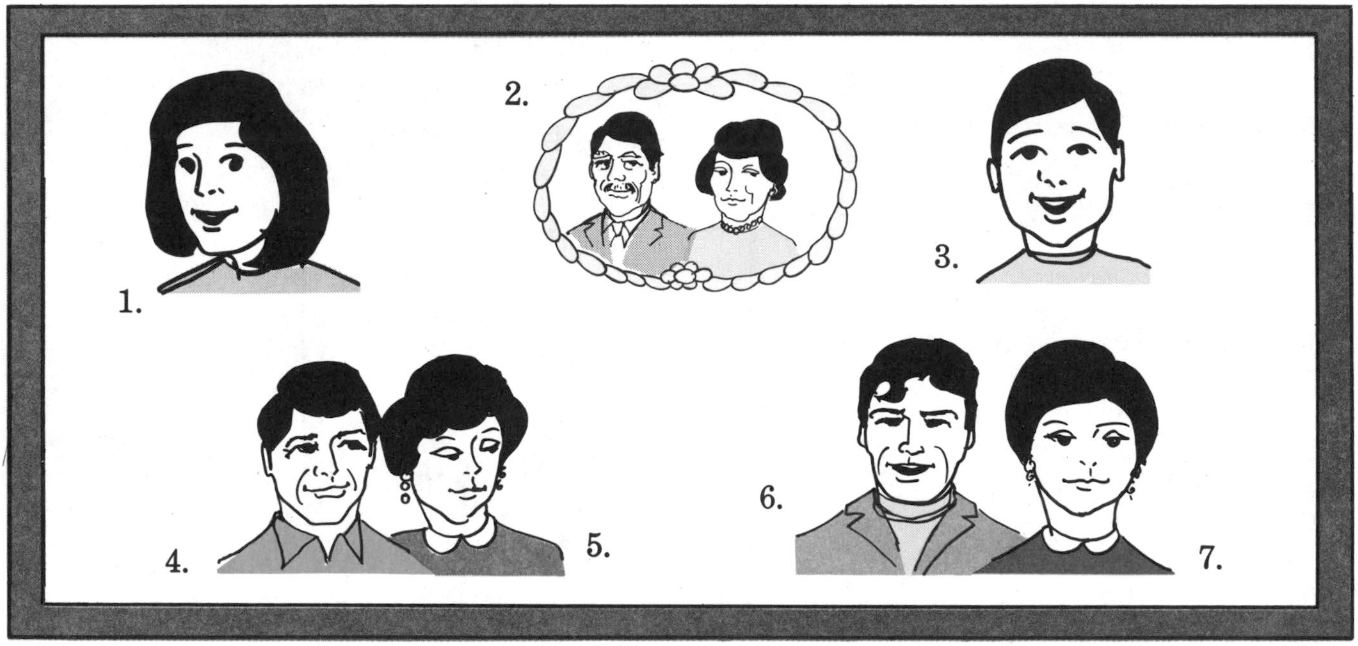

1. ____________
2. ____________
3. ____________
4. ____________
5. la zia
6. ____________
7. ____________

Don't be afraid of all the extra apostrophes and accents **in italiano.** Just concentrate on your easy pronunciation guide and remember: practice, practice, practice.

- ☐ **il motore** *(moh-toh-reh)* .... motor, engine
- ☐ **il momento** *(moh-men-toh)* .... moment
  - **—Un momento!** .... Just a moment!
- ☐ **la montagna** *(mohn-tahn-yah)* .... mountain
- ☐ **il museo** *(moo-seh-oh)* .... museum

(eem-pah-rah-reh)
Imparare!
to learn

Step 11

(leh-ee) **Lei** (you) have already used the verbs (ah-veh-reh) **avere** (to have) and (voh-reh-ee) **vorrei,** (would like) (koh-stah-reh) **costare,** (to cost) (ahr-ree-vah-reh) **arrivare,** (to arrive) (ehn-trah-reh) **entrare,** (to enter) (veh-nee-reh) **venire,** (to come) (ree-spohn-deh-reh) **rispondere,** (to respond) (ree-peh-teh-reh) **ripetere,** (to repeat) (eh) **è** (is) and (soh-noh) **sono.** (are) Although you might be able to "get by" **con** these (vehr-bee) **verbi,** let's assume you want to do (mehl-yoh) **meglio** (better) than that. First, a quick review.

How do you say **"I"** **in italiano?** io How do you say **"we"** **in italiano?** ______

Compare these **due** charts very carefully **e** (eem-pah-ree) **impari** (learn) these **sei parole.**

I	=	(ee-oh) **io**
he	=	(loo-ee) **lui**
she	=	(leh-ee) **lei**

we	=	(noh-ee) **noi**
you	=	(leh-ee) **Lei**
they	=	(loh-roh) **loro**

Adesso draw **linee** (frah) **fra** (between) the matching **parole** (een-gleh-see) **inglesi** **e parole** (ee-tah-lee-ah-neh) **italiane** below to see if (leh-ee) **Lei** (you) can keep these **parole** straight in your mind.

Note: **Lei,** with a capital "l" means you; **lei,** with a lower case "l," means she.

lei	he
loro	she
noi	I
Lei	they
io	we
lui	you

Adesso close **il libro e** write out both columns of the above practice on **un** (fohl-yoh) **foglio di** (piece) (kahr-tah) **carta.** (paper) How did (leh-ee) **Lei** do? (beh-neh) **Bene** (good) **o** (mah-leh) **male?** (bad) (nohn) **Non** (not) **bene** (good) **o non** (not) **male?** (bad) **Adesso** that **Lei** know these **parole,** you will soon be able to say almost anything (keh) **che** (that) **Lei** (deh-see-deh-rah) **desidera** (desire) by using a type of "plug-in" formula.

- ☐ **la musica** *(moo-see-kah)* .... music ______
- ☐ **nativo** *(nah-tee-voh)* .... native ______
- ☐ **naturale** *(nah-too-rah-leh)* .... natural ______
- ☐ **la nazione** *(nah-tsee-oh-neh)* .... nation, country ______
- ☐ **necessario** *(neh-chehs-sah-ree-oh)* .... necessary ______

To demonstrate, here are *(seh-ee)* **sei esempi** of some very practical **e** important **verbi italiani.** **These are verbi** whose basic form ends in "**are.**" Write **i verbi** in the blanks below after **Lei** have practiced them out loud many times.

(pahr-lah-reh) **parlare** = to speak	*(reh-stah-reh)* **restare** = to remain/stay	*(ah-bee-tah-reh)* **abitare** = to live/reside
______________	restare	______________
(ohr-dee-nah-reh) **ordinare** = to order	*(kohm-prah-reh)* **comprare** = to buy	*(kee-ah-mahr-see)* **chiamarsi** = to be called
______________	______________	______________

Study the following verb patterns **con** *(aht-tehn-tsee-oh-neh)* **attenzione.**
attention

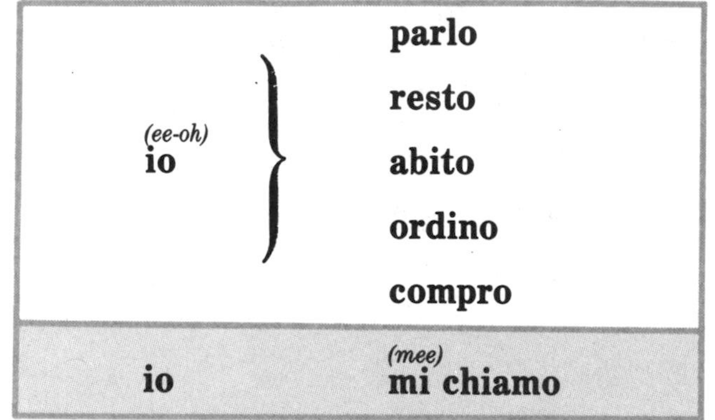

(ee-oh) **io**	**parlo** **resto** **abito** **ordino** **compro**
io	*(mee)* **mi chiamo**

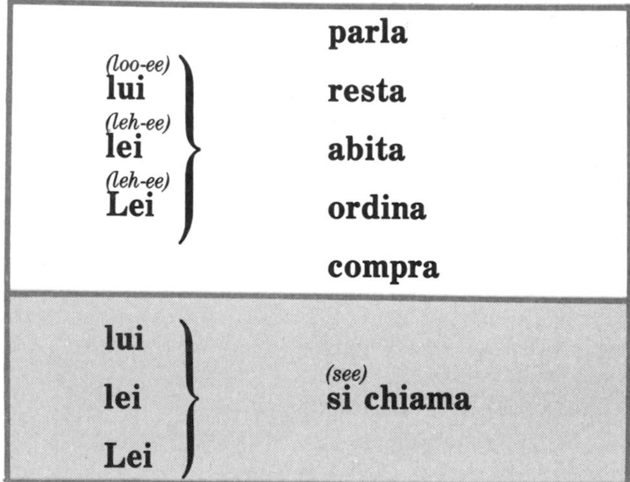

(loo-ee) **lui** *(leh-ee)* **lei** *(leh-ee)* **Lei**	**parla** **resta** **abita** **ordina** **compra**
lui **lei** **Lei**	*(see)* **si chiama**

Note:
- With **io,** you drop the final "**are**" from the basic verb form and add an "**o.**"
- With **lui, lei** and **Lei,** you simply drop the final "**are**" and add "**a.**"
- *(kee-ah-mahr-see)* **Chiamarsi** varies but not too much. It is a very important verb, so take a few extra minutes to learn it.

*Some **verbi italiani** will not conform to the rules quite as easily as these **verbi** do. But don't worry . . . you will be perfectly understood whether you say "**parlo**" or "**parla.**" *(l-yee)* **Gli** (the) **Italiani** will be delighted that you have taken the time to learn their language.

- ☐ **il nome** *(noh-meh)* .... name ______________
- ☐ **nord** *(nord)*................................ north ______________
- ☐ **normale** *(nor-mahl-leh)*................... normal ______________
- ☐ **la notizia** *(noh-tee-tsee-ah)* .... news, notice ______________
- ☐ **nuovo** *(noo-oh-voh)* .... new ______________

Note: • With **noi,** you drop the final **"are"** from the basic verb form and add **"iamo."**

Esempio: noi parliamo.
we speak

• With **loro,** you drop the final **"are"** and add **"ano."**

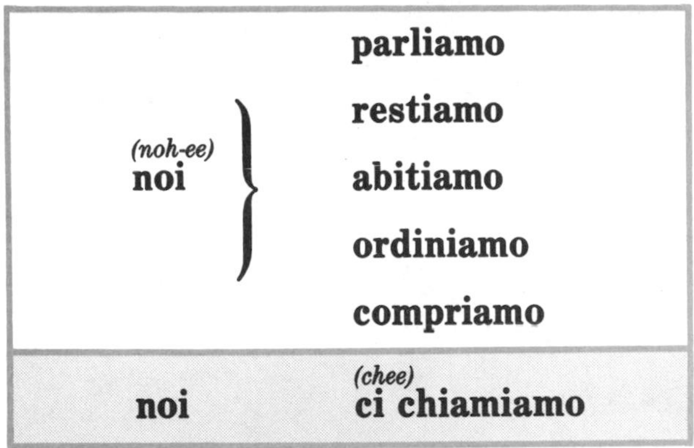

(noh-ee) **noi**	**parliamo** **restiamo** **abitiamo** **ordiniamo** **compriamo**
noi	*(chee)* **ci chiamiamo**

(loh-roh) **loro**	**parlano** **restano** **abitano** **ordinano** **comprano**
loro	**si chiamano**

Here are a few hints for mixing and matching **verbi** and their subjects.

-iamo ⟶ noi	ex.	**noi parliamo**
-o ⟶ io	ex.	**io parlo**
-ano ⟶ loro	ex.	**loro parlano**

Adesso, read through the entire verb form aloud several times before writing out each form in the blank below.

(pahr-lah-reh)
parlare
to speak

Io parlo **italiano.**
Lui / **Lei** (she) parla **italiano.**
Noi parliamo **italiano.**
Lei (you) parla **inglese.**
Loro parlano **inglese.**

(reh-stah-reh)
restare
to remain/stay

Io resto **in Italia.**
Lui / **Lei** (she) resta **in America.**
Noi restiamo **in Europa.**
Lei (you) resta **nell'albergo.**
Loro restano **in Francia.**

- ☐ **l'occasione** *(lohk-kah-see-oh-neh)* .... occasion, opportunity ______
- ☐ **occupato** *(ohk-koo-pah-toh)* .... occupied, busy ______
- ☐ **l'odore** *(loh-doh-reh)* .... odor ______
- ☐ **l'oggetto** *(loh-jet-toh)* .... object ______
- ☐ **l'ombrello** *(lohm-brel-loh)* .... umbrella ______

(ah-bee-tah-reh)
abitare
to live/reside

Io abito/ **in Italia.**

Lui ______ **in America.**
Lei (she)

Noi ______ **in** *(een-gheel-tehr-rah)* **Inghilterra.** England

Lei (you) ______ **in Europa.**

Loro ______ **in** *(chee-nah)* **Cina.** China

(kee-ah-mahr-see)
chiamarsi
to be called

Io mi chiamo/ **Maria Sandini.**

Lui si chiama/ **Mauro.**
Lei

Noi ci chiamiamo/ **Smith.**

Lei si chiama/ **Martini.**

Loro si chiamano/ **Verdi.**

(kohm-prah-reh)
comprare
to buy

Io compro/ **un libro.**

Lui ______ **un'insalata.**
Lei

Noi ______ **una macchina.**

Lei ______ **un orologio.**

Loro ______ **una lampada.**

(or-dee-nah-reh)
ordinare
to order

Io ordino/ **un** *(beek-kee-eh-reh)* **bicchiere di acqua.**

Lui ______ **un bicchiere di vino.**
Lei

Noi ______ **una tazza di tè.**

Lei ______ **una tazza di caffè.**

Loro ______ **bicchiere di** *(laht-teh)* **latte.** milk

Remember these **verbi?**

(veh-nee-reh) **venire** = to come
venire

(ahn-dah-reh) **andare** = to go
______

(eem-pah-rah-reh) **imparare** = to learn
______

(voh-reh-ee) **vorrei** = would like
______

(ah-veh-reh) **avere** = to have
______

(ah-veh-reh) **avere** to have *(bee-sohn-yoh)* **bisogno** need *(dee)* **di** of = to need
______

Here we have *(seh-ee)* **sei,** already familiar **verbi** whose following forms might seem a bit erratic after our last group. DON'T PANIC or give up. Read them out loud, practice them, think of their *(see-mee-lee-too-dee-nee)* **similitudini,** similarities write them out and *(poh-ee)* **poi** then try to use them in sentences of your own.

- ☐ **l'opera** *(loh-peh-rah)* .... opera ______
- ☐ **l'ora** *(loh-rah)* .... hour, time ______
- ☐ **ordinario** *(ohr-dee-nah-ree-oh)*............ ordinary ______
- ☐ **l'ospedale** *(loh-speh-dah-leh)* .... hospital ______
- ☐ **ovest** *(oh-vest)* .... west ______

Think of how hard it would be to speak **in inglese** with no verbs—it's the same **in italiano.**

(veh-nee-reh)
venire
to come

Io vengo ______ **dall'America.**

Lui viene ______ **dall'Inghilterra.**
Lei (she)

Noi veniamo ______ **dal Canada.** *(kah-nah-dah)*

Lei (you) viene ______ **da Nuova York.**

Loro vengono ______ **da Roma.** *(roh-mah)* Rome

(ahn-dah-reh)
andare
to go

Io vado ______ **in Italia.**

Lui va ______ **in Francia.** *(frahn-chah)* France
Lei (she)

Noi andiamo ______ **in Spagna.** *(spahn-yah)* Spain

Lei (you) va ______ **in Europa.**

Loro vanno ______ **in Cina.**

(eem-pah-rah-reh)
imparare
to learn

Io imparo ______ **l'italiano.**

Lui ______ **l'inglese.**
Lei

Noi ______ **la geometria.** *(jeh-oh-meh-tree-ah)* geometry

Lei ______ **il tedesco.** *(teh-deh-skoh)* German

Loro ______ **il francese.** *(frahn-cheh-seh)*

(voh-reh-ee)
vorrei
would like

Io vorrei ______ **un bicchiere di vino.**

Lui vorrebbe ______ **un bicchiere di vino rosso.**
Lei

Noi vorremmo ______ **un bicchiere di vino bianco.**

Lei vorrebbe ______ **un bicchiere di latte.**

Loro vorrebbero ______ **un bicchiere di birra.**

(ah-veh-reh)
avere
to have

Io ho ______ **mille lire.**

Lui ha ______ **due mila lire.**
Lei

Noi abbiamo ______ **cento lire.**

Lei ha ______ **cinquecento lire.**

Loro hanno ______ **cento mila lire.**

(ah-veh-reh) (bee-sohn-yoh) (dee)
avere bisogno di
to have need of

Io ho bisogno di ______ **una camera.** *(kah-meh-rah)* room

Lui ha bisogno di ______ **una camera.**
Lei

Noi abbiamo bisogno di ______ **una camera.**

Lei ha bisogno di ______ **una camera.**

Loro hanno bisogno di ______ **una camera.**

- ☐ **il pacco** *(pahk-koh)* . . . . package ______
- ☐ **il paio** *(pah-ee-oh)* . . . . pair ______
- **— un paio di scarpe** . . . . a pair of shoes ______
- ☐ **il palazzo** *(pah-lah-tsoh)* . . . . palace, building ______
- ☐ **i pantaloni** *(pahn-tah-loh-nee)* . . . . pants, trousers ______

Adesso take a deep breath. See if *(leh-ee)* **Lei** can fill in the blanks below. **Le risposte corrette sono** at the bottom of **la pagina.**

1. I speak Italian. ______________________________
2. He comes from America. ______________________________
3. We learn Italian. ______________________________
4. They have 1000 lire. ______________________________
5. She would like a glass of water. ______________________________
6. We need a room. Abbiamo bisogno di una camera.
7. My name is Paul Smith. ______________________________
8. I live in America. ______________________________
9. You are buying a book. ______________________________
10. He orders a beer. ______________________________

In the following Steps, **Lei** will be introduced to more **e** more **verbi e** should drill them in exactly the same way as **Lei** did in this section. Look up **le parole** *(noo-oh-veh)* **nuove** in your *(dee-tsee-oh-nah-ree-oh)* **dizionario** (dictionary) **e** make up your own sentences using the same type of pattern. Try out your **parole nuove** for that's how you make them yours to use on your holiday. Remember, the more **Lei** practice **adesso,** the more enjoyable your trip will be. **Buona fortuna!**

Adesso is a perfect time to turn to the back of **il libro,** clip out your flash cards **e** start flashing.

Be sure to check off your free **parole** in the box provided as **Lei** *(eem-pah-rah)* **impara** (learn) each one. 

RISPOSTE

1. **Io parlo italiano.**
2. **Lui viene dall'America.**
3. **Noi impariamo l'italiano.**
4. **Loro hanno mille lire.**
5. **Lei vorrebbe un bicchiere di acqua.**
6. **Noi abbiamo bisogno di una camera.**
7. **Mi chiamo Paul Smith.**
8. **Io abito in America.**
9. **Lei compra un libro.**
10. **Lui ordina una birra.**

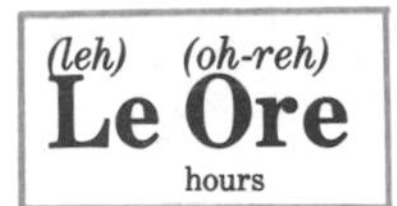

Lei know how to tell **i** *(johr-nee)* **giorni** (days) **della settimana** (week) **e i mesi** (months) **dell'anno,** (year) so **adesso** let's learn to tell time. As a *(vee-ah-jah-toh-reh)* **viaggiatore** (traveler) **in Italia, Lei** need to be able to tell time for *(preh-noh-tah-tsee-oh-nee)* **prenotazioni** (reservations)**, appuntamenti e treni. Ecco** the "basics."

What time is it? = **Che** *(oh-rah)* **ora è?** ______________________

half past	=	*(meh-zoh)* **e mezzo**	________
less	=	*(meh-noh)* **meno**	meno
midnight	=	*(meh-zah-noht-teh)* **mezzanotte**	________
noon	=	*(meh-zoh-johr-noh)* **mezzogiorno**	________

Sono le (it is) *(cheen-kweh)* **cinque.** (five o'clock)

Sono le quattro e mezzo.

Sono le tre.

Sono le due e mezzo.

È *(meh-zoh-johr-noh)* **mezzogiorno.**

Sono le otto e venti.

Sono le sette e quaranta. **O** **Sono le otto** (eight) **meno** (minus) **venti.** (twenty)

Adesso fill in the blanks according to **l'ora** indicated **sull'** (on the) **orologio.**

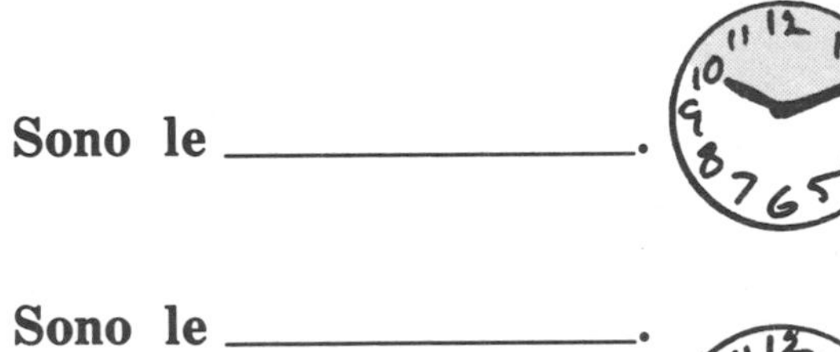

Sono le ______________.

Sono le ______________.

Sono le ______________.

Sono le ______________.

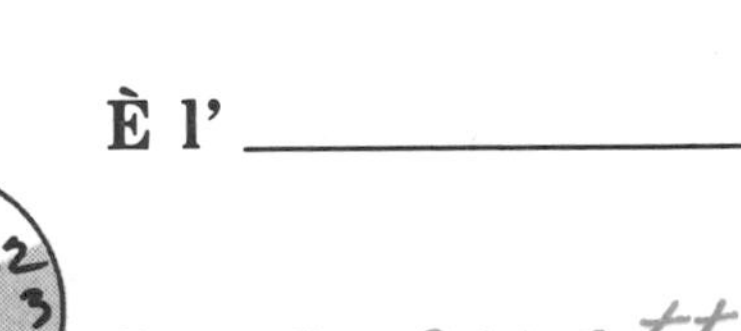

È l' ______________.

Sono le quattro.

Sono le ______________.

Sono le ______________.

RISPOSTE

Sono le due e venti.
Sono le sette e mezzo.
Sono le sei e dieci.

È l'una e mezzo.
Sono le quattro.
È mezzogiorno (o mezzanotte) e venti.
Sono le sei meno dieci.
(Sono le cinque e cinquanta.)

Ecco more time-telling *(pah-roh-leh)* **parole** to add to your *(pah-roh-lah)* **parola** power.

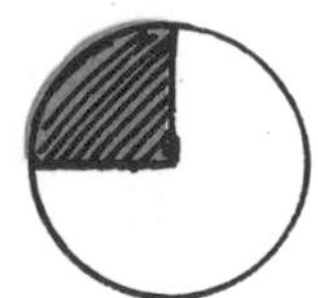

(kwahr-toh) **un quarto**	=	a quarter
(meh-noh) **meno un quarto**	=	a quarter to
e un quarto	=	a quarter past

Sono le due e un quarto. (it is) **O** **Sono le due e quindici.**

Sono le due meno un quarto. **O** **È l'una e quarantacinque.**

Adesso, your turn.

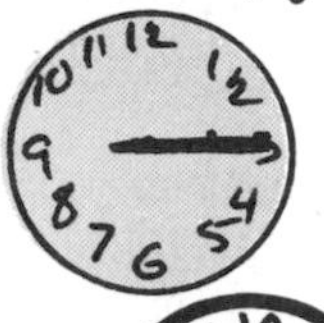

Sono le tre e un quarto .

Sono le ____________________ .

Sono le ____________________ .

Sono le ____________________ .

I numeri — see how **importanti** they have become! **Adesso, risponda alle domande** *(seh-gwen-tee)* **seguenti** (following) based on **gli orologi** below.

Che ora è?

1. ____________________
2. Sono le sette e mezzo.
3. ____________________
4. ____________________
5. ____________________
6. ____________________
7. ____________________

RISPOSTE

1. **Sono le sei.**
2. **Sono le sette e mezzo.**
3. **Sono le otto.**
4. **È l'una e mezzo.**
5. **È mezzogiorno (o mezzanotte) e un quarto.**
   È mezzogiorno (o mezzanotte) e quindici.
6. **Sono le nove e venti.**
7. **Sono le sei meno un quarto.**
   Sono le cinque e quarantacinque.

When **Lei** answer a "**quando**" *(kwahn-doh)* (when) question, say "**alle**" *(ah-leh)* (at) before you give the time.

TRENO 43 6:00

Quando arriva il treno? alle sei.

Adesso, risponda alle domande seguenti *(seh-gwen-tee)* (following) based on **gli** *(l-yee)* **orologi** below. Be sure to practice saying each question out loud several times.

Quando *(kwahn-doh)* **comincia** *(koh-meen-chah)* (begins) **il concerto?** *(kohn-chehr-toh)* (concert) ______________.

Quando comincia il film? *(feelm)* ______________.

Quando arriva l'autobus giallo? ______________.

Quando arriva il tassì? ______________.

Quando è aperto *(ah-pehr-toh)* (open) **il ristorante?** alle cinque.

Quando è chiuso *(kee-oo-soh)* (closed) **il ristorante?** ______________.

Alle *(ah-leh)* (at) **otto di** *(dee)* (in the) **mattina, si** *(see)* (one) **dice,** *(dee-cheh)* (says)

"Buon giorno, signora *(seen-yoh-rah)* (Mrs.) **Fellini."**

Alle otto di sera, si dice,

"Buona sera, signorina *(seen-yoh-ree-nah)* (Miss) **Bianchi."**

All'una del pomeriggio, si dice,

"Buon giorno, signor *(seen-yohr)* (Mr.) **Franchi."**

Alle dieci di sera, si dice,

"Buona notte."

- ☐ **il Papa** *(pah-pah)* .... Pope ______________
- ☐ **il parcheggio** *(pahr-keh-joh)* .... parking place, parking lot ______________
- ☐ **il parco** *(pahr-koh)* .... park ______________
- ☐ **Parigi** *(pah-ree-jee)* .... Paris ______________
- ☐ **la parte** *(pahr-teh)* .... part, portion ______________

Remember:

What time is it?	=	**Che ora è?**

When/at what time	=	**Quando?** **A che ora?**

Can **Lei** pronounce **e** understand **il** **paragrafo** *(pah-rah-grah-foh)* paragraph **seguente?** *(seh-gwen-teh)*

Il treno di Parigi arriva alle 15,15.

Sono adesso le 15,20. Il treno è in ritardo. *(ree-tahr-doh)* late **Il treno arriva oggi alle 17,15. Domani il treno arriva di** *(dee)* **nuovo** *(noo-oh-voh)* again **alle 15,15.**

Ecco more practice exercises. **Risponda alle domande** based on **l'ora** given.

Che ora è?

1. (1:30) ____________________
2. (6:30) ____________________
3. (2:15) *Sono le due e un quarto.*
4. (11:40) ____________________
5. (12:18) ____________________
6. (7:20) ____________________
7. (3:10) ____________________
8. (4:05) ____________________
9. (5:35) ____________________
10. (11:50) ____________________

Note: When writing the time, Italians use a comma instead of a colon to separate the hour from the minutes (*e.g.,* 7,30).

- ☐ **la partenza** *(pahr-ten-tsah)*............ departure ____________
- ☐ **il passaporto** *(pahs-sah-pohr-toh)*...... passport ____________
- ☐ **la pasta** *(pah-stah)*.................. pasta (**fettucine, ravioli,** etc.) ____________
- ☐ **la patata** *(pah-tah-tah)*.............. potato ____________
- ☐ **la penna** *(pen-nah)*................... pen ____________

Ecco a quick quiz. Fill in the blanks **con i numeri corretti. Le risposte sono sotto** *(soht-toh)* below**.**

1. **Un minuto** *(mee-noo-toh)* **ha** *(ah)* has ______ (?) **secondi** *(seh-kohn-dee)*.

2. **Un'ora ha** ______ (?) **minuti** *(mee-noo-tee)*.

3. **Un giorno ha** ______ (?) **ore.**

4. **Una settimana ha** ______ (?) **giorni** *(johr-nee)*.

5. **Un mese ha** trenta (?) **giorni.**

6. **Un anno ha** ______ (?) **mesi.**

7. **Un anno ha** ______ (?) **settimane.**

8. **Un anno ha** ______ (?) **giorni.**

Ecco a sample **pagina** from **un orario** *(oh-rah-ree-oh)* timetable **delle FS** *(eh-feh-eh-seh)*—the Italian national railroad. **Un rapido** *(rah-pee-doh)* **(RAP) e un espresso** *(es-pres-soh)* **(ESP) sono molto rapidi** *(rah-pee-dee)* fast**. Un diretto** *(dee-ret-toh)* **(DIR) e un direttissimo (DIR.MO) sono rapidi. Un accelerato** *(ah-cheh-leh-rah-toh)* **(ACC) è molto lento** *(len-toh)* slow and stops at every small station along the way.

MILANO—ROMA

Treno	Partenza	Arrivo
19 RAP	6,05	14,30
22 ACC	7,40	23,50
4 DIR.MO	9,45	20,32
50 ESP	11,10	18,20
10 DIR	23,00	9,05

RISPOSTE

1. **sessanta**
2. **sessanta**
3. **ventiquattro**
4. **sette**
5. **trenta**
6. **dodici**
7. **cinquantadue**
8. **trecento sessantacinque**

Ecco tre verbi nuovi *(pehr)* **per** (for) Step 12.

(dee-reh) **dire** = to say — *(mahn-jah-reh)* **mangiare** = to eat — *(beh-reh)* **bere** = to drink

dire ______ ______ ______

(dee-reh) **dire** (to say)

Io dico/ ______ **"Buon giorno."**

Lui / **Lei** (she) dice/ ______ **"Ciao."**

Noi diciamo/ ______ **"No."**

Lei (you) dice/ ______ **"Si."**

Loro non dicono/ ______ *(nee-ehn-teh)* **niente.** (nothing)

(mahn-jah-reh) **mangiare** (to eat)

Io mangio/ ______ **la** *(mee-neh-strah)* **minestra.** (soup)

Lui / **Lei** ______ **la** *(bee-stehk-kah)* **bistecca.** (beefsteak)

Noi ______ **molto.**

Lei non ______ *(nee-en-teh)* **niente.** (nothing)

Loro ______ **i** *(rah-vee-oh-lee)* **ravioli.**

(beh-reh) **bere** (to drink)

Io bevo/ ______ **il latte.**

Lui / **Lei** beve/ ______ **il vino bianco.**

Noi beviamo/ ______ **la birra.**

Lei beve/ ______ **un bicchiere di acqua.**

Loro bevono/ ______ **il tè.**

Have you noticed that, to make a plural **in italiano,** you don't add an **"s"** to the end of the word? Instead, the final **"o"** or **"e"** changes to **"i,"** and the final **"a"** changes to **"e."**

- ☐ **perfetto** *(pehr-fet-toh)*.................. perfect ______
- ☐ **il periodo** *(peh-ree-oh-doh)* .... period ______
- ☐ **la permanenza** *(pehr-mah-nen-tsah)*..... stay, permanence ______
- ☐ **il permesso** *(pehr-mehs-soh)* .... permission ______
- **— Permesso?**........................ May I pass through? ______

(kwah-droh)
il **quadro**

(sohf-fee-toh)
il **soffitto**

(lahn-goh-loh)
l'angolo

(fee-neh-strah)
la **finestra**

(lahm-pah-dah)
la **lampada**

(loo-cheh)
la **luce**

(soh-fah)
il **sofà**

(seh-dee-ah)
la **sedia**

(tahp-peh-toh)
il **tappeto**

(tah-voh-loh)
il **tavolo**

(pohr-tah)
la **porta**

(loh-roh-loh-joh)
l'orologio

(ten-dee-nah)
la **tendina**

(pah-reh-teh)
la **parete**

(kah-sah)
la **casa**

(sah-lah) (dah) (prahn-zoh)
la **sala da pranzo**

(sah-loht-toh)
il **salotto**

(kah-meh-rah) (dah) (let-toh)
la **camera da letto**

(stahn-zah) (dah) (bahn-yoh)
la **stanza da bagno**

(koo-chee-nah)
la **cucina**

(loof-fee-choh)
l'ufficio

(kahn-tee-nah)
la **cantina**

(gah-rahzh)
il **garage**

(lah-oo-toh)
l'auto

(mahk-kee-nah)
la **macchina**

(bee-chee-klet-tah)
la **bicicletta**

(kah-neh)
il **cane**

(gaht-toh)
il **gatto**

(jahr-dee-noh)
il **giardino**

(poh-stah)
la **posta**

(boo-kah) (del-leh) (let-teh-reh)
la **buca delle lettere**

(fee-oh-ree)
i **fiori**

(kahm-pah-nel-loh)
il **campanello**

(oo-noh)
1 uno

(doo-eh)
2 due

(treh)
3 tre

(kwaht-troh)
4 quattro

(cheen-kweh)
5 cinque

(seh-ee)
6 sei

(set-teh)
7 sette

(oht-toh)
8 otto

(noh-veh)
9 nove

(dee-eh-chee)
10 dieci

(bee-ahn-koh)
bianco

(neh-roh)
nero

(jahl-loh)
giallo

(rohs-soh)
rosso

(ah-zoor-roh)
azzurro

(gree-joh)
grigio

(mahr-roh-neh)
marrone

(vehr-deh)
verde

(roh-sah)
rosa

(mool-tee-koh-loh-reh)
multicolore

(loo-neh-dee)
lunedì

(mahr-teh-dee)
martedì

(mehr-koh-leh-dee)
mercoledì

(joh-veh-dee)
giovedì

(veh-nehr-dee)
venerdì

(sah-bah-toh)
sabato

(doh-meh-nee-kah)
domenica

(bwohn) (johr-noh)
buon giorno

(bwoh-nah) (seh-rah)
buona sera

(bwoh-nah) (noht-teh)
buona notte

(chah-oh)
ciao

(free-goh-ree-feh-roh)
il **frigorifero**

(koo-chee-nah)
la **cucina**

(vee-noh)
il **vino**

(beer-rah)
la **birra**

(laht-teh)
il **latte**

(boor-roh)
il **burro**

(pee-aht-toh)
il **piatto**

(sah-leh)
il **sale**

(peh-peh)
il **pepe**

(kohl-tel-loh)
il **coltello**

(tah-tsah)
la **tazza**

(fohr-ket-tah)
la **forchetta**

(bee-kee-eh-reh)
il **bicchiere**

(toh-vahl-yoh-loh)
il **tovagliolo**

(kook-kee-ah-ee-oh)
il **cucchiaio**

(lar-mah-dee-et-toh) (koo-chee-nah)
l'armadietto di cucina

STICKY LABELS

This book has over 150 special sticky labels for you to use as you learn new words. When you are introduced to a word, remove the corresponding label from these pages. Be sure to use each of these unique labels by adhering them to a picture, window, lamp, or whatever object it refers to. The sticky labels make learning to speak Italian much more fun and a lot easier than you ever expected.

For example, when you look in the mirror and see the label, say

(loh) *(spek-kee-oh)*
"lo specchio."

Don't just say it once, say it again and again.

And once you label the refrigerator, you should never again open that door without saying

(eel) *(free-goh-ree-feh-roh)*
" il frigorifero."

By using the sticky labels, you not only learn new words but friends and family learn along with you!

(pah-neh) il pane	(kahr-tah) la carta	(sah-poh-neh) il sapone	(lah-bee-toh) l'abito
(teh) il tè	(let-teh-rah) la lettera	(spah-tsoh-lee-noh) (dah) (den-tee) lo spazzolino da denti	(krah-vaht-tah) la cravatta
(kahf-feh) il caffè	(kahr-toh-lee-nah) la cartolina	(den-tee-free-choh) il dentifricio	(fah-tsoh-let-toh) il fazzoletto
(choh-koh-lah-toh) il cioccolato	(frahn-koh-bohl-loh) il francobollo	(pet-tee-neh) il pettine	(kah-mee-chah) la camicia
(lah-kwah) l'acqua	(lee-broh) il libro	(soh-prah-bee-toh) il soprabito	(jahk-kah) la giacca
(let-toh) il letto	(ree-vee-stah) la rivista	(leem-pehr-meh-ah-bee-leh) l'impermeabile	(pahn-tah-loh-nee) i pantaloni
(koh-pehr-tah) la coperta	(johr-nah-leh) il giornale	(lohm-brel-loh) l'ombrello	(veh-stee-toh) il vestito
(koo-shee-noh) il cuscino	(ohk-kee-ah-lee) gli occhiali	(gwahn-tee) i guanti	(kah-mee-chet-tah) la camicetta
(zvel-yah) la sveglia	(teh-leh-vee-zee-oh-neh) la televisione	(kahp-pel-loh) il cappello	(gohn-nah) la gonna
(lahr-mah-dee-oh) l'armadio	(cheh-stee-noh) il cestino	(stee-vah-lee) gli stivali	(mahl yah) la maglia
(lah-vahn-dee-noh) il lavandino	(pahs-sah-pohr-toh) il passaporto	(skahr-peh) le scarpe	(reh-jee-pet-toh) il reggipetto
(doh-chah) la doccia	(beel-yet-toh) il biglietto	(kahl-tsee-noh) il calzino	(soht-toh-veh-steh) la sottoveste
(vee-chee) il W.C.	(vah-lee-jah) la valigia	(kahl-tseh) le calze	(kah-noht-tee-eh-rah) la canottiera
(spehk-kee-oh) lo specchio	(bohr-sah) la borsa	(pee-jah-mah) il pigiama	(moo-tahn-deh) le mutande
(gwahn-toh) (dah) (bahn-yoh) il guanto da bagno	(pohr-tah-fohl-yoh) il portafoglio	(pahn-toh-foh-leh) le pantofole	(bwohn) (ahp-peh-tee-toh) buon appetito
(lah-shoo-gah-mah-noh) l'asciugamano	(deh-nah-roh) il denaro	(lahk-kahp-pah-toh-ee-oh) l'accappatoio	(ohk-koo-pah-toh) occupato
(lah-shoo-gah-mah-noh) (peek-koh-loh) l'asciugamano piccolo	(mahk-kee-nah) (foh-toh-grah-fee-kah) la macchina fotografica	(kah-mee-chah) (dah) (noht-teh) la camicia da notte	(mee) (skoo-see) mi scusi
(lah-shoo-gah-mah-noh) (bahn-yoh) l'asciugamano da bagno	(pel-lee-koh-lah) la pellicola	(soh-noh) (ah-meh-ree-kah-noh) Sono americano.	
(mah-tee-tah) la matita	(koh-stoo-meh) (dah) (bahn-yoh) il costume da bagno	(vohr-reh-ee) (eem-pah-rah-reh) (lee-tah-lee-ah-noh) Vorrei imparare l'italiano.	
(pen-nah) la penna	(sahn-dah-lee) i sandali	(mee) (kee-ah-moh) Mi chiamo _______________.	

PLUS . . .

Your book includes a number of other innovative features. At the back of the book, you'll find seven pages of flash cards. Cut them out and flip through them at least once a day.

On pages 112 and 113, you'll find a beverage guide and a menu guide. Don't wait until your trip to use them. Clip out the menu guide and use it tonight at the dinner table. And use the beverage guide to practice ordering your favorite drinks.

By using the special features in this book, you will be speaking Italian before you know it.

(nord) Nord - (sood) Sud, (est) Est - (oh-vest) Ovest
north - south, east - west

Step 13

If **Lei** are looking at **una** (kahr-tah) **carta** (map) (jeh-oh-grah-fee-kah) **geografica e Lei** see **le parole seguenti,** it should not be too (dee-fee-chee-leh) **difficile** (difficult) to figure out what they mean. Take an educated guess. **Le risposte sono sotto.**

(lah-meh-ree-kah) (del) (nord) **l'America del nord**	(lah-meh-ree-kah) (sood) **l'America del sud**	(kah-roh-lee-nah) **la Carolina del nord**
(mah-reh) **il Mare del nord**	(lah-free-kah) **l'Africa del sud**	(dah-koh-tah) **il Dakota del sud**
(leer-lahn-dah) **l'Irlanda del nord**	(kah-roh-lee-nah) **la Carolina del sud**	(tehr-ree-toh-ree) **i Territori del nord-ovest**
(dah-koh-tah) **il Dakota del nord**	(poh-loh) **il Polo sud**	(poh-loh) **il Polo nord**

Le parole italiane per north, south, east **e** west **sono** easy to recognize due to their **similitudini** to **inglese.** So . . .

(nord) **il nord**	=	the north	________
(sood) **il sud**	=	the south	il sud
(lest) **l'est**	=	the east	________
(loh-vest) **l'ovest**	=	the west	________

del nord	=	northern	________
del sud	=	southern	________
dell'est	=	eastern	dell'est
dell'ovest	=	western	________

These **parole sono molto importanti.** Learn them (oh-jee) **oggi.** But what about more basic (dee-reh-tsee-oh-nee) **direzioni** (directions) such as "left," "right," **e** "straight ahead"? Let's learn these **parole adesso.**

straight ahead	=	(dee-reet-toh) **diritto**
to the left	=	(ah) (see-nee-strah) **a sinistra**
to the right	=	(ah) (deh-strah) **a destra**

RISPOSTE

North America	South America	North Carolina
North Sea	South Africa	South Dakota
Northern Ireland	South Carolina	Northwest Territories
North Dakota	South Pole	North Pole

Just as **in inglese,** these **tre** *(frah-see)* **frasi** (phrases) go a long way.

(pehr) (fah-voh-reh) **per favore**	=	please
(grah-tsee-eh) **grazie**	=	thank you ~~grazie, grazie, grazie~~
(mee) (skoo-see) **mi scusi**	=	excuse me

Ecco due *(kohn-vehr-sah-tsee-oh-nee)* **conversazioni** *(tee-pee-keh)* **tipiche** (typical) **per** someone who is trying to find something.

Gianni: **Mi scusi,** *(mah)* **ma** (but) **dov'è l'Albergo Florio?**

Pietro: *(kohn-tee-noo-ee)* **Continui diritto,** *(poh-ee)* **poi** (then) *(jee-ree)* **giri** (turn) **a sinistra alla** *(seh-kohn-dah)* **seconda** (second) *(strah-dah)* **strada** (street) **e l'Albergo Florio è** *(lee)* **lì** (there) **a destra.**

Gianni: **Mi scusi, Signore. Dov'è la Villa Giulia?**

Pietro: **Giri** (turn) *(kwee)* **qui** (here) **a destra, continui diritto** *(pehr)* **per** (for) **cento** *(meh-tree)* **metri** (meters) *(pee-oo)* **più** (more) **o** (or) *(meh-noh)* **meno,** (less) **e poi giri a sinistra e la Villa Giulia è** *(ahl-lahn-goh-loh)* **all'angolo.** (at the corner)

Are you lost? There is no need to be lost if **Lei** *(ah)* **ha** (have) learned the basic **parole di** *(dee-reh-tsee-oh-neh)* **direzione.** (direction) Do not try to memorize these **conversazioni** because you will never be looking for precisely these places. One day you might need to ask for **direzioni** to **"il** *(foh-roh)* **Foro** *(roh-mah-noh)* **Romano,"** (the Roman Forum) **"la** *(tor-reh)* **Torre** *(pen-den-teh)* **Pendente"** (the Leaning Tower) **o "il** *(koh-lohs-seh-oh)* **Colosseo."** (the Colosseum) Learn the key **parole di direzione e** be sure **Lei** can find your *(deh-stee-nah-tsee-oh-neh)* **destinazione.** (destination)

What if the person responding to your **domanda** answers too quickly for you to understand the entire reply? If so, ask again, saying,

- ☐ **la persona** *(pehr-soh-nah)* .... person ____________
- ☐ **il pezzo** *(peh-tsoh)* .... piece ____________
- ☐ **il piacere** *(pee-ah-cheh-reh)* .... pleasure ____________
  - **— per piacere** .... if you please ____________
  - **— Molto piacere** .... "It's a pleasure to meet you." ____________

Mi scusi. Sono americano e parlo (soh-lah-men-teh) **solamente** (only) **un** (poh-koh) **poco** (little) **d'italiano. Parli** (pee-oo) **più** (more) (len-tah-men-teh) **lentamente** (slowly) **per favore, e ripeta** (lah) **la** (soo-ah) **Sua** (your) **risposta. Molte** (many) **grazie** (thanks).

Adesso, quando the directions are repeated, **Lei** will be able to understand if (leh-ee) **Lei** (ah) **ha** (have) learned the key **parole** for **direzioni** (directions). Quiz yourself by filling in the blanks **sotto con le parole corrette in italiano.**

Stefano: **Mi scusi, Signorina. Dov'è il ristorante** (ahl-freh-doh) **"Alfredo"?**

Anna: (dah) **Da** (from) (kwee) **qui** (here)**, continui** ________ (straight ahead)**; poi, alla** (tehr-zah) **terza** (third) strada (street), **giri** a ________ (right). (cheh) **C'è** (there is) **una chiesa.** (soo-bee-toh) **Subito** (immediately) (doh-poh) **dopo** (after) ________ (the church), ________ (turn) (dee) **di** (noo-oh-voh) **nuovo** (again) ________ (right) **e il ristorante "Alfredo" è** ________ (on the left), all'angolo (on the corner). **Buona fortuna.**

Ecco quattro verbi nuovi.

(ah-spet-tah-reh) **aspettare**	= to wait for	aspettare, aspettare
(kah-pee-reh) **capire**	= to understand	________
(ven-deh-reh) **vendere**	= to sell	________
(ree-peh-teh-reh) **ripetere**	= to repeat	________

- ☐ **il piatto** *(pee-aht-toh)* .... plate, dish ________
- ☐ **la piazza** *(pee-ah-tsah)* .... plaza, town square ________
- ☐ **la pillola** *(peel-loh-lah)* .... pill ________
- ☐ **pittoresco** *(peet-toh-reh-skoh)* .... picturesque ________
- ☐ **la polizia** *(poh-lee-tsee-ah)* .... police ________

As always, say each sentence out loud. Say each and every **parola** carefully, pronouncing each Italian sound as well as **Lei** can.

(ah-spet-tah-reh)
aspettare
to wait for

Io ______________ **il treno.**

Lui
Lei ______________ **l'autobus.**

Noi ______________ **davanti all'albergo.**

Lei ______________ **il tassì.**

Loro ______________ **molti** *(mohl-tee)* many **biglietti.**

(kah-pee-reh)
capire
to understand

Io ______________ **l'inglese.**

Lui
Lei ______________ **l'italiano.**

Noi ______________ **l'italiano.**

Lei ______________ **il menù** *(meh-noo)* menu**.**

Loro ______________ **il russo** *(roos-soh)* Russian**.**

(ven-deh-reh)
vendere
to sell

Io ______________ **dei fiori.**

Lui
Lei ______________ **della frutta** *(fruht-tah)* fruit**.**

Noi ______________ **un cappotto** *(kahp-poht-toh)* overcoat**.**

Lei ______________ **una macchina.**

Loro ______________ **molti** *(mohlt-tee)* many **biglietti.**

(ree-peh-teh-reh)
ripetere
to repeat

Io ______________ **la parola.**

Lui
Lei ______________ **la risposta.**

Noi ______________ **i nomi.**

Lei ______________ **la lezione** *(leh-tsee-oh-neh)* lesson**.**

Loro ______________ **il verbo.**

Adesso, see if **Lei** can translate the following thoughts **in italiano. Le risposte sono sotto.**

Note: **Lei** don't need to use these pronouns **in italiano, Lei** can just use **i verbi.**

1. She repeats the word. ______________
2. They sell many tickets. ______________
3. He waits for the taxi. ______________
4. We eat some fruit. ______________
5. I speak Italian. ______________
6. I drink a cup of tea. ______________

RISPOSTE

1. **Lei ripete la parola.** **(Ripete la parola.)**
2. **Loro vendono molti biglietti.** **(Vendono molti biglietti.)**
3. **Lui aspetta il tassì.** **(Aspetta il tassì.)**
4. **Noi mangiamo della frutta.** **(Mangiamo della frutta.)**
5. **Io parlo italiano.** **(Parlo italiano.)**
6. **Io bevo una tazza di tè.** **(Bevo una tazza di tè.)**

Di Sopra - Di Sotto

(dee) (soh-prah) (dee) (soht-toh)
above below

Step 14

Before **Lei comincia** (koh moon chah) [begin] Step 14, review Step 8. **Adesso impariamo ancora** (ahn-koh-rah) [more] **delle parole.**

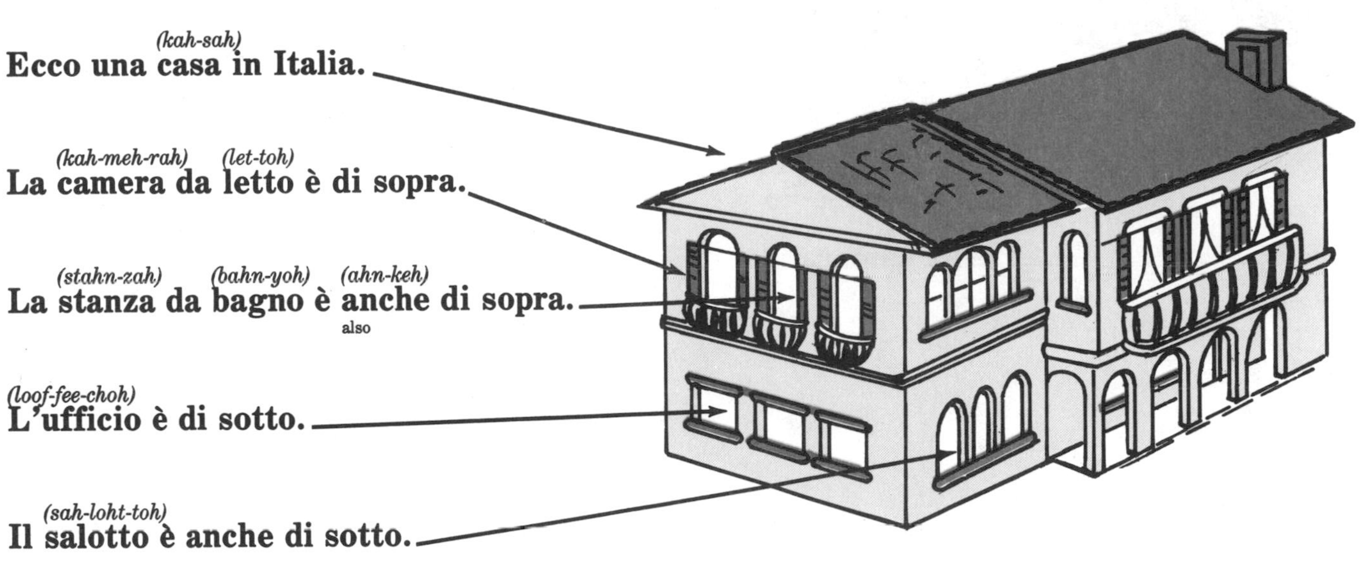

Vada (vah-dah) [go] **adesso in** your **camera da letto e** look around **la stanza.** Let's learn **i nomi delle** [of the] **cose nella** [in the] **camera,** just as **abbiamo** learned the various parts of **la casa.** Be sure to practice saying **le parole** as **Lei** write them in the spaces **sotto.** Also say out loud the example sentences **sotto le illustrazioni.**

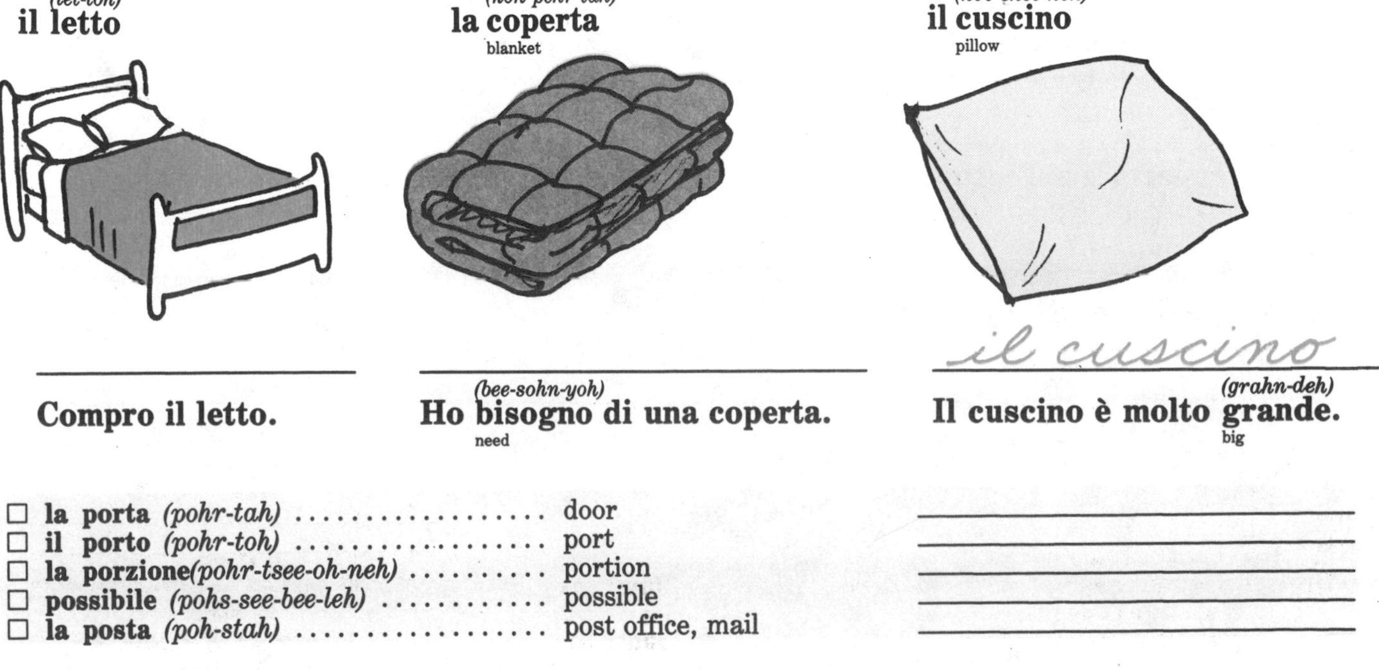

- ☐ **la porta** *(pohr-tah)* .... door ______
- ☐ **il porto** *(pohr-toh)* .... port ______
- ☐ **la porzione** *(pohr-tsee-oh-neh)* .... portion ______
- ☐ **possibile** *(pohs-see-bee-leh)* .... possible ______
- ☐ **la posta** *(poh-stah)* .... post office, mail ______

(zvel-yah)
la sveglia

(lahr-mah-dee-oh)
l'armadio

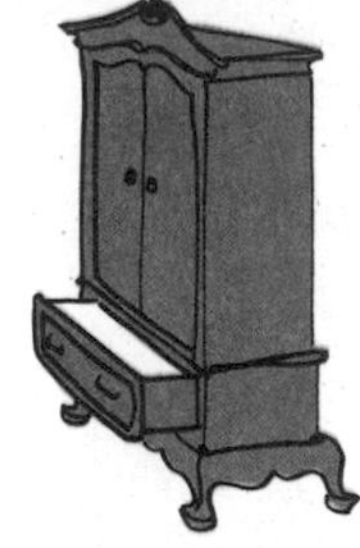

Remove the next **cinque** stickers **e** label these **cose in** your **camera da letto.**

Ho una sveglia.

(cheh)
C'è un armadio (there is) **nella camera.**

La camera nell'albergo o nell'ostello (oh-stel-loh) (hostel) **della gioventù** (joh-ven-too) (youth) is for sleeping. **dormire** (dohr-mee-reh) = to sleep. This is **un verbo importante per il viaggiatore** (vee-ah-jah-toh-reh) (traveler) **stanco.** (stahn-koh) (tired) Study **le domande e le risposte seguenti** based on **l'illustrazione a sinistra.**

1. Dov'è la sveglia?

La sveglia è sul tavolo.

2. Dov'è la coperta?

La coperta è sul letto.

3. Dov'è l'armadio?

L'armadio è nella camera.

4. Dov'è il cuscino?

Il cuscino è sul letto.

5. Dov'è il letto?

Il letto è nella camera.

6. Il letto è grande (grahn-deh) (big) **o piccolo?** (peek-koh-loh) (small)

Il letto non (nohn) (not) **è grande.**

Il letto è piccolo.

- ☐ **povero** *(poh-veh-roh)* .... poor
- ☐ **precedente** *(preh-cheh-den-teh)*.......... preceding
- ☐ **preciso** *(preh-chee-soh)* .... precise, exact
  - **— alle sei preciso** .... at six o'clock on the dot
- ☐ **presente** *(preh-sen-teh)*................ present

Adesso, risponda alle domande based on the previous **illustrazione.**

Dov'è la *(zvel-yah)* **sveglia?**

Dov'è il letto?

La sveglia è ______________________ ______________________

Let's move into **la stanza da bagno e** do the same thing.

il *(lah-vahn-dee-noh)* **lavandino**

il lavandino

C'è un lavandino nella stanza da bagno.

la *(doh-chah)* **doccia**

____

La doccia non è nella camera dell'albergo.

il *(vee-chee)* **W.C.**

____

Il W.C. non è (is not) **nella camera dell'albergo. Il W.C. e la doccia sono nel** *(kohr-ree-doh-ee-oh)* **corridoio** (hallway).

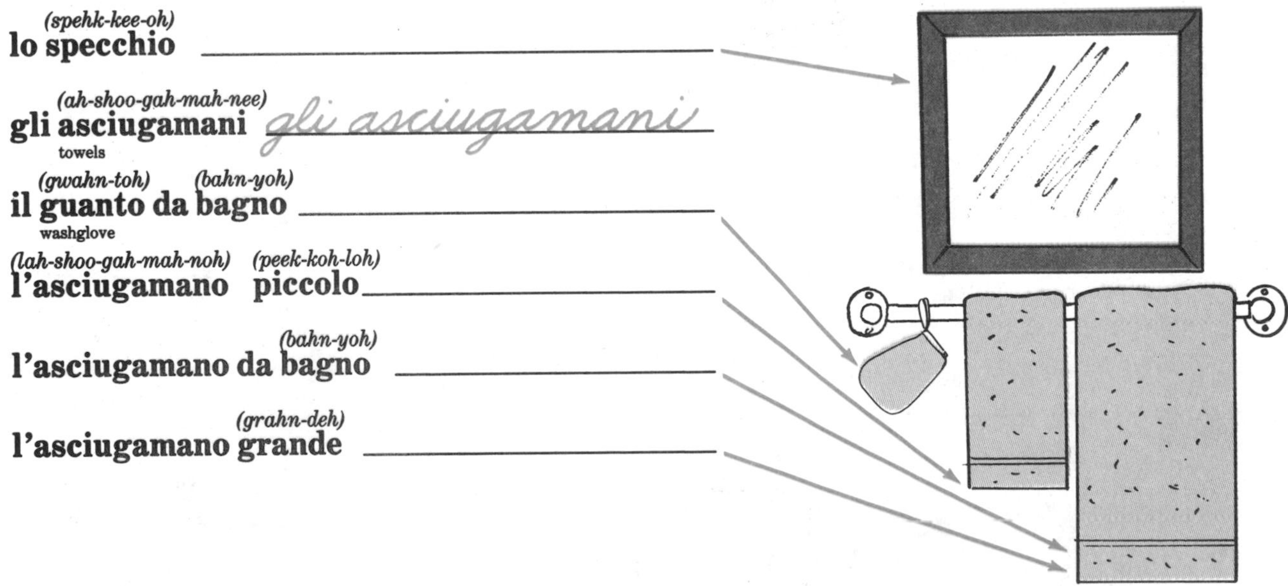

lo *(spehk-kee-oh)* **specchio** ______________________

gli *(ah-shoo-gah-mah-nee)* **asciugamani** (towels) *gli asciugamani*

il *(gwahn-toh)* **guanto da** *(bahn-yoh)* **bagno** (washglove) ______________________

(lah-shoo-gah-mah-noh) **l'asciugamano** *(peek-koh-loh)* **piccolo** ______________________

l'asciugamano da *(bahn-yoh)* **bagno** ______________________

l'asciugamano *(grahn-deh)* **grande** ______________________

Do not forget to remove **i otto** stickers **seguenti e** label these **cose in** your **stanza da bagno.**

- ☐ **prezioso** *(preh-tsee-oh-soh)* .... precious, valuable ______________________
- ☐ **il prezzo** *(preh-tsoh)* .... price ______________________
- ☐ **il problema** *(proh-bleh-mah)* .... problem ______________________
- ☐ **pronto** *(prohn-toh)* .... prompt, ready ______________________
  - **—"Pronto!"** .... "Hello!" (answering telephone) ______________________

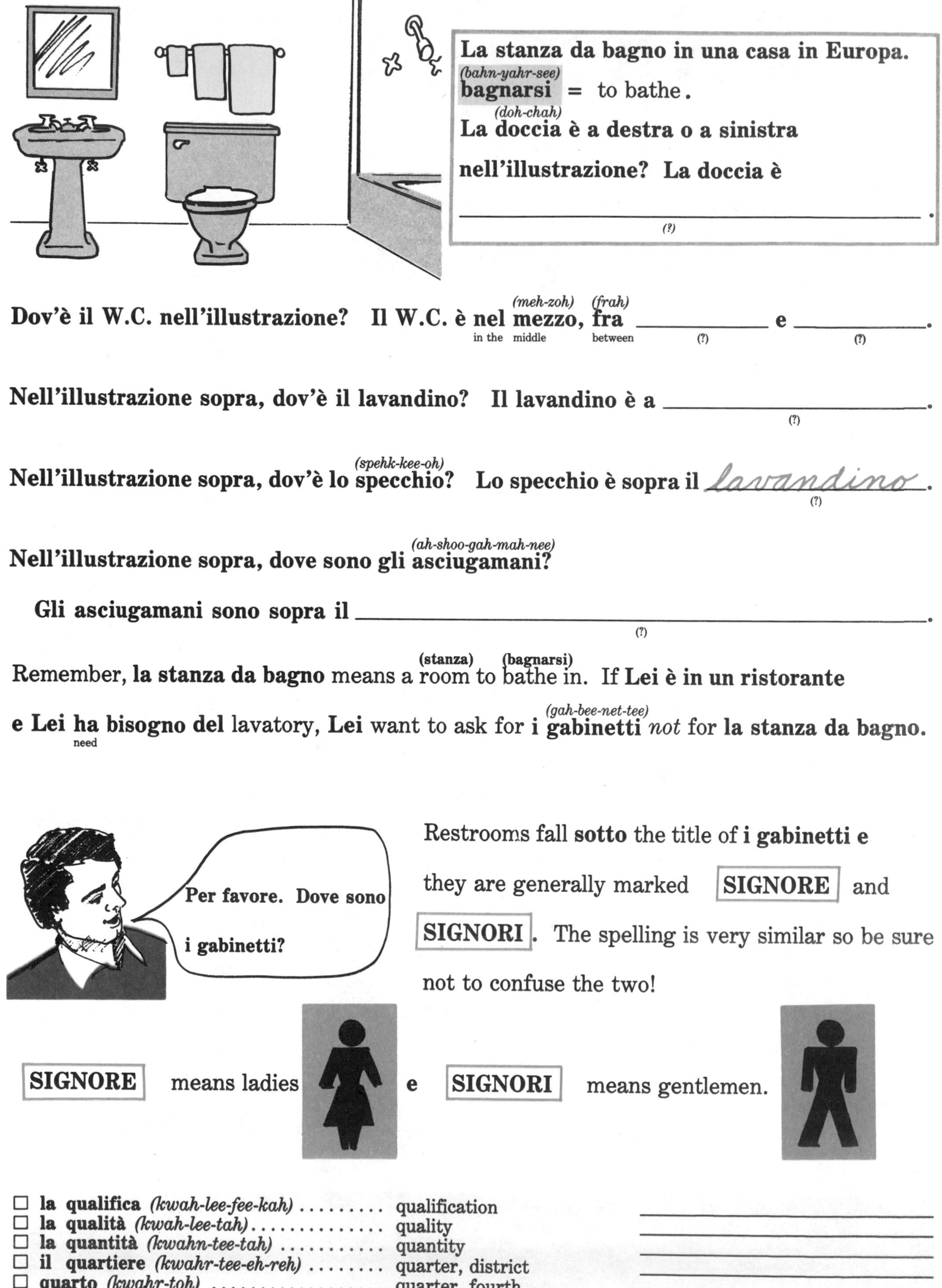

La stanza da bagno in una casa in Europa.

bagnarsi *(bahn-yahr-see)* = to bathe.

La doccia *(doh-chah)* **è a destra o a sinistra nell'illustrazione? La doccia è** ______________________ (?).

Dov'è il W.C. nell'illustrazione? Il W.C. è nel (in the) **mezzo** *(meh-zoh)* (middle), **fra** *(frah)* (between) ____________ (?) **e** ____________ (?).

Nell'illustrazione sopra, dov'è il lavandino? Il lavandino è a ______________________ (?).

Nell'illustrazione sopra, dov'è lo specchio *(spehk-kee-oh)*? **Lo specchio è sopra il** lavandino (?).

Nell'illustrazione sopra, dove sono gli asciugamani *(ah-shoo-gah-mah-nee)*?

Gli asciugamani sono sopra il ______________________ (?).

Remember, **la stanza da bagno** means a room (stanza) to bathe (bagnarsi) in. If **Lei è in un ristorante e Lei ha** (need) **bisogno del** lavatory, **Lei** want to ask for **i gabinetti** *(gah-bee-net-tee)* *not* for **la stanza da bagno.**

Restrooms fall **sotto** the title of **i gabinetti e** they are generally marked **SIGNORE** and **SIGNORI**. The spelling is very similar so be sure not to confuse the two!

SIGNORE means ladies **e** **SIGNORI** means gentlemen.

- ☐ **la qualifica** *(kwah-lee-fee-kah)* .... qualification ______
- ☐ **la qualità** *(kwah-lee-tah)* .... quality ______
- ☐ **la quantità** *(kwahn-tee-tah)* .... quantity ______
- ☐ **il quartiere** *(kwahr-tee-eh-reh)* .... quarter, district ______
- ☐ **quarto** *(kwahr-toh)* .... quarter, fourth ______

Next stop — **l'ufficio** *(loof-fee-choh)*, specifically, **il tavolo** (table) **o la scrivania** *(skree-vah-nee-ah)* (desk) **nell'ufficio. Che** *(keh)* **c'è** *(cheh)* (is there) **sulla scrivania?** Let's identify **le cose** one normally finds **nell'ufficio** *(oof-fee-choh)* **o** strewn about **la casa.**

la matita *(mah-tee-tah)*	**la penna** *(pen-nah)*	**la carta** *(kahr-tah)*	**la lettera** *(let-teh-rah)*

____________	la penna	____________	____________
la cartolina *(kahr-toh-lee-nah)*	**il francobollo** *(frahn-koh-bohl-loh)*	**il libro** *(lee-broh)*	**la rivista** *(ree-vee-stah)* magazine
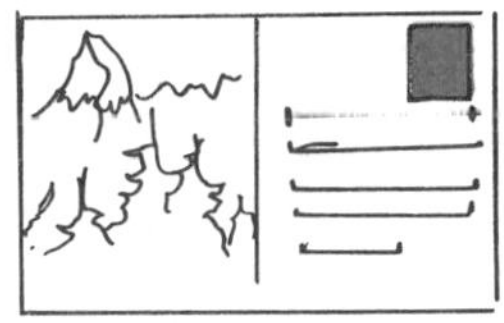			
____________	____________	____________	____________
il giornale *(johr-nah-leh)*	**gli occhiali** *(ohk-kee-ah-lee)*	**la televisione** *(teh-leh-vee-zee-oh-neh)*	**il cestino** *(cheh-stee-noh)*

____________	____________	____________	____________

- ☐ **la radio** *(rah-dee-oh)* .... radio ____________
- ☐ **la ragione** *(rah-joh-neh)* .... reason ____________
- ☐ **rapido** *(rah-pee-doh)* .... rapid, fast ____________
- ☐ **recente** *(reh-chehn-teh)* .... recent ____________
- ☐ **il resto** *(reh-stoh)* .... rest, change (from money) ____________

Adesso, label these **cose nell'ufficio con** your stickers. Do not forget to say these **parole** out loud whenever **Lei le** *(leh)* (them) **scrive,** *(skree-veh)* (write) **Lei** see them **o Lei** apply the stickers. **Adesso,** identify **le cose sotto** by filling in each blank **con la parola corretta in italiano.**

1. ____________________
2. ____________________
3. ____________________
4. ____________________
5. la matita
6. ____________________
7. ____________________
8. ____________________
9. ____________________
10. ____________________

Ecco quattro verbi di *(dee)* **più** *(pee-oo)* (more)**.**

(veh-deh-reh) **vedere** = to see	*(mahn-dah-reh)* **mandare** = to send	*(dohr-mee-reh)* **dormire** = to sleep	*(troh-vah-reh)* **trovare** = to find
____________	____________	dormire	____________

Adesso, fill in the blanks, **alla** (on) **prossima** *(prohs-see-mah)* (next) **pagina, con la forma corretta** of these **verbi.**

Practice saying the sentences out loud many times.

- ☐ **ricco** *(reek-koh)* . . . . rich ____________
- ☐ **la ricetta** *(ree-cheht-tah)* . . . . recipe ____________
- ☐ **il ricordo** *(ree-kohr-doh)* . . . . souvenir, record ____________
- ☐ **il Rinascimento** *(ree-nah-shee-men-toh)* . . . . . Renaissance ____________
- ☐ **il rispetto** *(ree-speht-toh)* . . . . respect ____________

(veh-deh-reh)
vedere
to see

Io vedo **il letto.**

Lui / Lei ______ **la coperta.**

Noi ______ **l'albergo.**

Lei ______ **il** *(koh-lohs-seh-oh)* **Colosseo.** (Colosseum)

Loro ______ **la doccia.**

(mahn-dah-reh)
mandare
to send

Io ______ **la lettera.**

Lui / Lei ______ **la cartolina.**

Noi ______ **il libro.**

Lei ______ **quattro cartoline.**

Loro mandano **tre lettere.**

(dohr-mee-reh)
dormire
to sleep

Io ______ **nella camera.**

Lui / Lei dorme **nel letto.**

Noi ______ **nell'albergo.**

Lei ______ **nella casa.**

Loro ______ **sotto la coperta.**

(troh-vah-reh)
trovare
to find

Io ______ **il francobollo.**

Lui / Lei ______ **i giornali.**

Noi troviamo **gli occhiali.**

Lei ______ **la** *(gohn-doh-lah)* **gondola.** (Venetian boat)

Loro ______ **i fiori.**

The expressions *(veh-roh)* **"vero"** o **"non è vero"** are useful **in italiano.** When added to the end of a sentence, the sentence becomes a question for which **la risposta** is usually **"sí."** Compare them to their equivalents **in inglese.**

È un libro, vero?	=	It's a book, isn't it?
Sofia è bella, non è vero?	=	Sophia is beautiful, isn't she?
Lei è italiano, vero?	=	You're Italian, aren't you?
Mandiamo molte cartoline, non è vero?	=	We send lots of postcards, don't we?

- ☐ **il ristorante** *(ree-stoh-rahn-teh)* .... restaurant ______
- ☐ **ritardo** *(ree-tahr-doh)* .... late ______
- ☐ **la rivista** *(ree-vee-stah)* .... magazine, review ______
- ☐ **Roma** *(roh-mah)*..................... Rome ______
- ☐ **la rosa** *(roh-sah)* .... rose ______

Step 15

Lei know **adesso** how to count, how to ask **domande,** how to use **verbi con** the "plug-in" formula, how to make statements, **e** how to describe something, be it the location of **un albergo o il colore di una casa.** Let's now take the basics that **Lei ha** learned **e** expand them in special areas that will be most helpful in your travels. What does everyone do on a holiday? Send postcards, (nohn) (eh) (veh-roh) **non è vero?** (don't they) Let's learn exactly how (loof-fee-choh) (poh-stah-leh) **l'ufficio postale italiano (PT)** works.

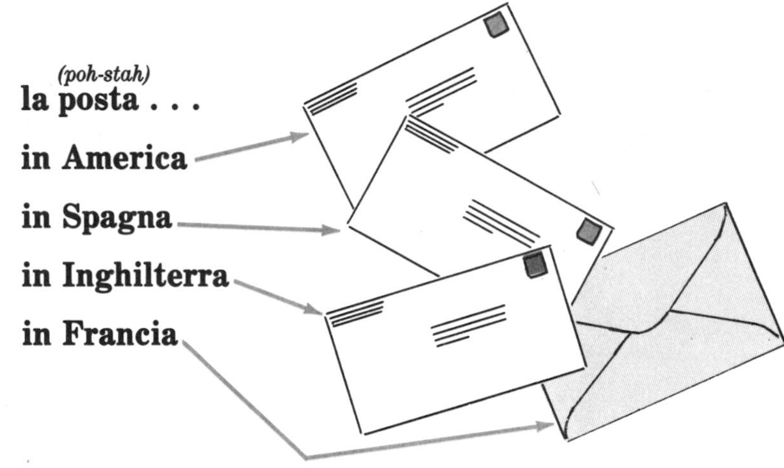

The (pee-tee) (poh-steh) **PT** (post office) **(Poste e Telegrafi)** is where **Lei** need to go **in Italia** to buy stamps, mail a package or send a telegram. **(Lei** may also buy stamps and stationery at the (sah-lee) **Sali e** (tah-bahk-kee) **Tabacchi**—salt and tobacco store—of which there are many.) **Ecco** some **parole necessarie per l'ufficio postale.**

(let-teh-rah) **la lettera**	(kahr-toh-lee-nah) **la cartolina**	(frahn-koh-bohl-loh) **il francobollo**	(teh-leh-grahm-mah) **il telegramma**
	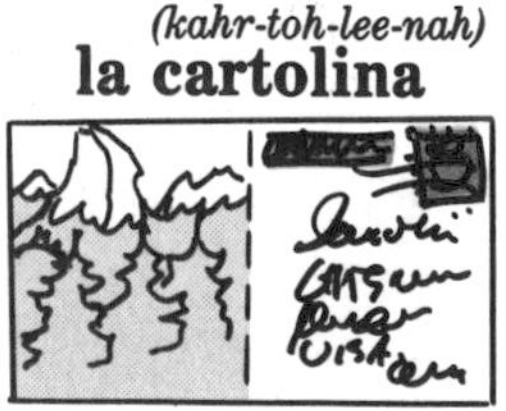		

la lettera ____________ ____________ ____________

- ☐ **il sacco** *(sahk-koh)* .... sack, bag ____________
- ☐ **il sale** *(sah-leh)* .... salt ____________
  - **—Sali e Tabacchi** .... salt and tobacco store ____________
- ☐ **la salsa** *(sahl-sah)* .... sauce ____________
- ☐ **il saluto** *(sah-loo-toh)* .... greeting, salutation ____________

(pahk-koh)
il pacco

(boo-kah) (del-leh) (let-teh-reh)
la buca delle lettere

(vee-ah)(ah-eh-reh-ah)
via aerea

(spohr-tel-loh)
lo sportello
ticket window

________ ________ via aerea ________

(kah-bee-nah)(teh-leh-foh-nee-kah)
la cabina telefonica

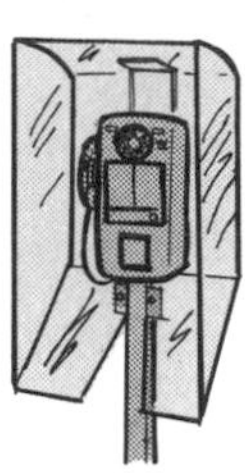

(teh-leh-foh-noh)
il telefono

(pee-tee) (loof-fee-choh) (poh-stah-leh)
le PT /l'ufficio postale

________ ________ ________

Le PT in Italia sono importanti. Lei manda *(mahn-dah)* (send) **i telegrammi, le lettere, le cartoline e i pacchi** *(pahk-kee)* **dall'ufficio postale. Lei compra i francobolli nell'ufficio postale. L'ufficio postale è generalmente** *(jeh-neh-rahl-men-teh)* open from **le 8,00 di mattina alle 2,00 del pomeriggio** weekdays, **e le 8,00 alle 12,00 il sabato** *(sah-bah-toh)* (Saturday)**. Il Lei ha bisogno** to call home **in America,** this can be done **all'ufficio postale e** is called **una telefonata** *(teh-leh-foh-nah-tah)* (call) **interurbana** *(een-tair-oor-bah-nah)* (long-distance)**.** (within Italy.)

Okay. First step — enter **le PT.**

The following **è una buona** *(bwoh-nah)* sample **conversazione.** Familiarize yourself **con queste** *(kweh-steh)* (these) **parole adesso.**

- ☐ **la scala** *(skah-lah)* .... staircase, stairs ________
- **—la Scala** .... Milanese opera house ________
- ☐ **lo scavo** *(skah-voh)* .... excavation ________
- ☐ **la scena** *(sheh-nah)* .... scene ________
- ☐ **la scienza** *(shee-en-zah)* .... science ________

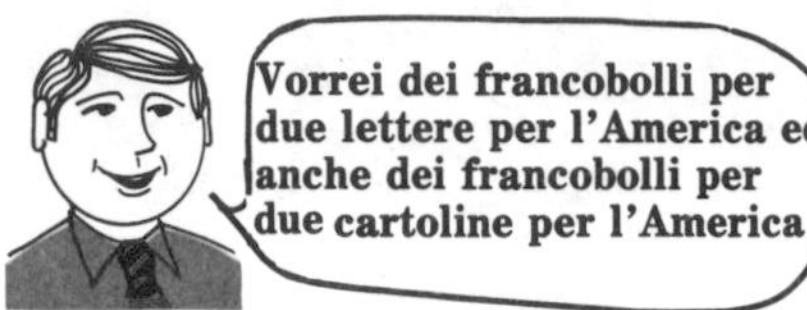

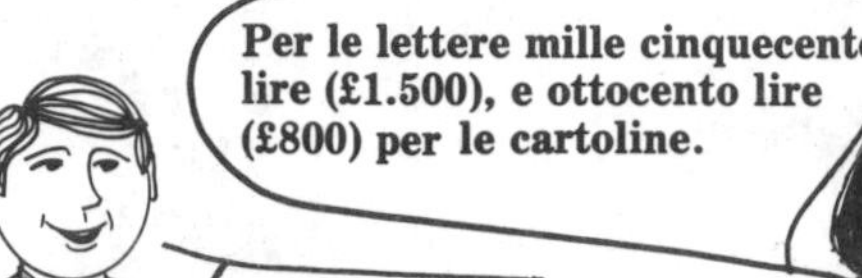

Sí, via aerea, per favore. Vorrei anche dei francobolli per due lettere per l'Italia. Quanto costa?

Bene.

Molte grazie, Signorina.

Next step — **Lei** ask **domande** (questions) like those **sotto** depending upon what **Lei vorrebbe** *(vor-rehb-beh)* (would like).

Dove compro (I buy) **i francobolli?**

Dove compro una cartolina?

Dove faccio *(fah-choh)* (I make) **una telefonata** *(teh-leh-foh-nah-tah)* (telephone call)**?**

Dove faccio una telefonata interurbana *(een-tair-oor-bah-nah)***?**

Dov'è l'ufficio postale?

Dove mando (I send) **un telegramma?**

Dove mando un pacco?

Dov'è la cabina telefonica?

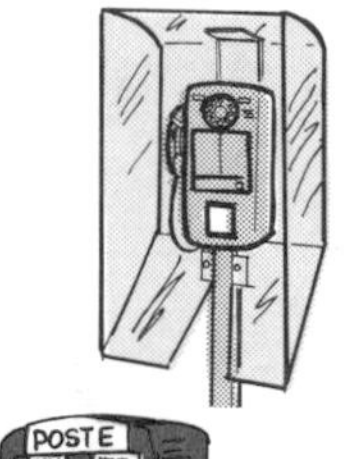

Quanto costa?

Dov'è la buca delle lettere?

Ripeta many times **queste** *(kwehs-teh)* (these) **frasi di sopra. Adesso,** quiz yourself. See if **Lei** can translate the following thoughts **in italiano. Le risposte sono** at the bottom of **la prossima** *(prohs-see-mah)* (next) **pagina.**

1. Where is a telephone booth? ______________________
2. Where do I make a phone call? Dove si telefona?
3. Where is the mailbox? ______________________
4. Where do I make a long-distance phone call? ______________________
5. Where is the post office? ______________________

- ☐ **secondo** *(seh-kohn-doh)* .... second ______________
- ☐ **il segnale** *(sen-yah-leh)* .... signal, sign ______________
- ☐ **il segretario** *(seh-greh-tah-ree-oh)* ...... secretary ______________
- ☐ **la selezione** *(seh-leh-tsee-oh-neh)* .... selection, choice ______________
- ☐ **la semisfera** *(seh-mee-sfeh-rah)* .... hemisphere ______________

6. Where does one buy stamps? ____________________

7. How much is it? ____________________

8. Where does one send a package? ____________________

9. Where does one send a telegram? ____________________

10. Where is window eight? ____________________

Ecco quattro verbi nuovi.

(fah-reh) **fare** = to do/make   *(moh-strah-reh)* **mostrare** = to show   *(skree-veh-reh)* **scrivere** = to write   *(pah-gah-reh)* **pagare** = to pay

__________   __________   scrivere   __________

(fah-reh) **fare** to do/make

Io faccio/ ____________ **una telefonata.**

Lui / Lei fa/ ____________ **il letto.**

Noi facciamo/ ____________ **molto.**

Lei non fa/ ____________ *(nee-ehn-teh)* **niente.** nothing

Loro fanno/ ____________ *(too-toh)* **tutto.** everything

(skree-veh-reh) **scrivere** to write

Io ____________ **una lettera.**

Lui / Lei scrive/ ____________ **molto.** a lot

Noi ____________ **un telegramma.**

Lei ____________ *(leen-dee-ree-tsoh)* **l'indirizzo.** address

Loro ____________ **niente.**

(moh-strah-reh) **mostrare** to show

Io ____________ **il libro.**

Lui / Lei le (to you) ____________ **l'ufficio.**

Noi le (to you) ____________ *(pah-lah-tsoh)* **il palazzo.**

Lei mi (to me) mostra/ ____________ **la lettera.**

Loro mi ____________ **le PT.**

(pah-gah-reh) **pagare** to pay

Io ____________ *(kohn-toh)* **il conto.** bill

Lui / Lei ____________ *(tahs-sah)* **la tassa.** tax

Noi paghiamo/ ____________ **il giornale.**

Lei ____________ *(preh-tsoh)* **il prezzo.** price

Loro non ____________ **niente.**

RISPOSTE

6. Dove si comprano i francobolli?
7. Quanto costa?
8. Dove si manda un pacco?
9. Dove si manda un telegramma?
10. Dov'è lo sportello numero otto?

1. Dov'è la cabina telefonica?
2. Dove si telefona?
3. Dov'è la buca delle lettere?
4. Dove si fa una telefonata interurbana?
5. Dov'è l'ufficio postale?

Step 16

Come *(koh-meh)* Pagare *(pah-gah-reh)*
how — to pay

Sì, ci *(chee)* [there are] **sono anche** [also] bills to pay **in Italia. Lei** have just finished your **pasto** *(pah-stoh)* [meal] **squisito** *(skwee-see-toh)* [delicious] **e Lei vorrebbe** *(vor-rehb-beh)* [would like] **il conto e Lei vorrebbe pagare. Che fa Lei? Lei** call for **il cameriere** *(kah-meh-ree-eh-reh)* [waiter] **o la cameriera** *(kah-meh-ree-eh-rah)* [waitress].

Il cameriere *(kah-meh-ree-eh-reh)* will normally reel off what **Lei ha** eaten, while writing rapidly. **Lui** will then place **un piccolo** *(peek-koh-loh)* [little] **foglio** *(fohl-yoh)* [sheet] **di carta sulla tavola** that looks like **il conto nell'illustrazione,** while saying something like:

"Fa tredici mila lire, Signore."
it makes

Lei will pay **il cameriere** or perhaps **Lei** will pay **alla cassa** *(kahs-sah)* [cashier's desk]. Tipping **in Italia** is the same as tipping **in America.** Generally, **Lei** should leave a 15-percent **mancia** *(mahn-chah)* [tip] **sulla tavola.**

Sometimes **Lei** will notice that **il servizio** *(sehr-vee-tsee-oh)* is included on **il conto,** which means **la mancia** has already been added on to **il conto** by **il ristorante.** In this case, **Lei** should not leave another **mancia.**

- ☐ **semplice** *(sehm-plee-cheh)* .... simple, easy ________________
- ☐ **il sentimento** *(sen-tee-men-toh)* .... feeling ________________
- ☐ **serio** *(seh-ree-oh)* .... serious ________________
- ☐ **il servizio** *(sehr-vee-tsee-oh)* .... service ________________
- ☐ **sfortunato** *(sfor-too-nah-toh)* .... unfortunate ________________

Remember these key **parole** when dining out *(ahl-lee-tah-lee-ah-nah)* **all'italiana.** (in the Italian manner)

(meh-noo) **il menù** or *(lee-stah)* **la lista**	*(mahn-chah)* **la mancia**
(kohn-toh) **il conto**	

La *(jehn-tee-leh-tsah)* **gentilezza** (politeness) **è molto importante in Italia.** You will feel more **italiano** if you practice and use *(kweh-steh)* **queste** (these) *(es-pres-see-oh-nee)* **espressioni.** (expressions)

mi scusi

per favore or **per** *(pee-ah-cheh-reh)* **piacere**

grazie or **molte grazie**

(preh-goh) **prego** (you're welcome)

Ecco una sample **conversazione** involving paying **il conto** when leaving **un albergo.**

Gianni:	**Mi scusi, Signore.** *(voh-reh-ee)* **Vorrei pagare il conto, per favore.**
(lahl-behr-gah-toh-reh) L'albergatore: (hotelkeeper)	*(keh)* **Che** (what) **camera, per favore?**
Gianni:	**Numero trecento dieci.**
L'albergatore:	**Grazie. Un momento, per piacere.**
	Ecco il conto. Fa quindici mila duecento lire.
Gianni:	**Molte grazie (e Gianni** hands him **un biglietto da venti mila lire.** **L'albergatore** returns shortly **e** *(dee-cheh)* **dice.)** (says)
L'albergatore:	**Ecco la Sua** (your) *(ree-cheh-voo-tah)* **ricevuta** (receipt) **e il** *(reh-stoh)* **resto** (change) **(4.800 lire). Grazie e** *(ahr-ree-veh-dehr-chee)* **arrivederci.** (good-bye)

Simple, right? If **Lei ha** any **problema con i numeri,** just ask someone to write out **la** *(sohm-mah)* **somma** (sum) so that **Lei** can be sure you understand everything correctly.

Per favore, *(mee)* **mi** (for me) *(skree-vah)* **scriva** (write) **la somma** (sum)**. Grazie.**

Let's take a break from **il denaro e,** starting **alla** *(prohs-see-mah)* **prossima** (next) **pagina,** learn some **nuove** fun **parole.**

- ☐ **sicuro** *(see-koo-roh)* .... sure, safe, secure ______________
- ☐ **il sidro** *(see-droh)* .... cider ______________
- ☐ **la sigaretta** *(see-gah-ret-tah)*.......... cigarette ______________
- ☐ **il sigaro** *(see-gah-roh)*................ cigar ______________
- ☐ **simile** *(see-mee-leh)* .... similar ______________

È in buona *(sah-loo-teh)* **salute.** health

È *(mah-lah-toh)* **malato.** sick

È *(bwoh-noh)* **buono.** good

Non è buono.

È *(kaht-tee-voh)* **cattivo.** bad

L'acqua è *(kahl-dah)* **calda.** warm

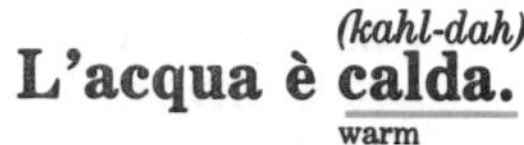

Sono 50 gradi.

L'acqua è *(frehd-dah)* **fredda.** cold

Sono 17 gradi.

FORTE!

piano

Lei parla *(for-teh)* **forte.** loudly

Noi parliamo *(pee-ah-noh)* **piano.** softly

La linea rossa è *(kohr-tah)* **corta.** short

La linea azzurra è *(loon-gah)* **lunga.** long

La donna è *(grahn-deh)* **grande.**

Il bambino è *(peek-koh-loh)* **piccolo.**

Il libro rosso è *(grohs-soh)* **grosso.** thick

Il libro verde è *(soht-tee-leh)* **sottile.** thin

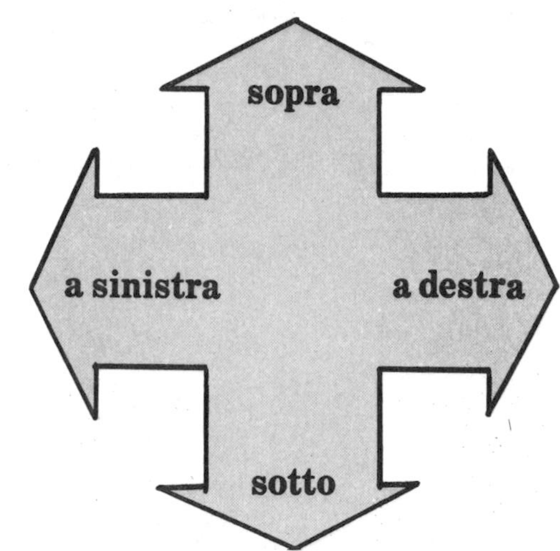

20 *(kee-loo-meh-tree)* **chilometri** all'ora per hour

(len-toh) **lento** slow

200 chilometri all'ora

(veh-loh-cheh)(rah-pee-doh) **veloce / rapido** fast

- ☐ **sincero** *(seen-cheh-roh)* .... sincere
- ☐ **la sinfonia** *(seen-foh-nee-ah)*........... symphony
- ☐ **il soggetto** *(soh-jet-toh)*................ subject
- ☐ **solo** *(soh-loh)* .... alone, solitary
- ☐ **la somma** *(sohm-mah)* .... total, sum

Le montagne sono alte (ahl-teh) high. Sono alte 2000 metri (meh-tree) meters.

Le montagne sono basse (bahs-seh) low. Sono alte solamente (soh-lah-men-teh) only 800 metri.

Il nonno è vecchio (vek-kee-oh) old. Ha (ah) he has settanta anni (ahn-nee) years.

Il bambino è giovane (joh-vah-neh) young. Ha solamente dieci anni.

La camera dell'albergo è cara (kah-rah) expensive. Costa 50.000 lire.

La camera dell'ostello (oh-stehl-loh) hostel della gioventù (joh-ven-too) youth è economica (eh-koh-noh-mee-kah) inexpensive.

Costa 5.000 lire.

Ho 500.000 lire. Sono ricco (reek-koh) rich. È molto (mohl-toh) much denaro.

Lui ha solamente 200 lire. È povero (poh-veh-roh) poor. È poco (poh-koh) little denaro.

Ecco dei (deh-ee) some verbi nuovi.

sapere (sah-peh-reh) = to know (a fact, an address, etc.)

potere (poh-teh-reh) = to be able to/can

dovere (doh-veh-reh) = to have to/ to owe

leggere (leh-jeh-reh) = to read

_______________ _______________ dovere _______________

I verbi "**sapere**," "**potere**," "**dovere**," along with "**volere**," can be joined with another **verbo**:

Sappiamo (we know how) **trovare** (to find) **l'indirizzo** (the address).
Sappiamo parlare italiano.

Possiamo (we can) **parlare** (speak).
Possiamo capire (understand).

Dobbiamo (we must) **pagare** (pay).
Dobbiamo mangiare (eat).

- ☐ **la sorpresa** *(sohr-preh-sah)* .... surprise _______________
- ☐ **lo spagnolo** *(spahn-yoh-loh)* .... Spanish, Spaniard _______________
- ☐ **lo spettacolo** *(speht-tah-koh-loh)* .... spectacle, show _______________
- ☐ **gli Stati Uniti** *(stah-tee) (oo-nee-tee)* .... United States _______________
- ☐ **lo straniero** *(strah-nee-eh-roh)* .... stranger, foreigner _______________

Study their pattern closely as **Lei** will use **molto** (a lot) **questi** *(kweh-stee)* (these) **verbi.**

(sah-peh-reh)
sapere
to know

Io so/ **tutto.** (everything)

Lui / Lei sa/ **l'indirizzo.**

Noi sappiamo/ **parlare italiano.**

Lei sa/ **ordinare una birra.**

Loro sanno/ **l'indirizzo.**

(poh-teh-reh)
potere
to be able to/can

Io posso/ **parlare italiano.**

Lui / Lei può/ **capire l'inglese.**

Noi possiamo/ **bere.**

Lei può/ **entrare.**

Loro possono/ **parlare italiano anche.**

(doh-veh-reh)
dovere
to have to/owe

Io devo/ **pagare il conto.**

Lui / Lei deve/ **restare all'albergo.**

Noi dobbiamo/ **visitare** *(vee-see-tah-reh)* (to visit) **Roma.**

Lei ci *(chee)* (to us) deve/ **100 lire.**

Loro devono/ **pagare il conto.**

(leh-jeh-reh)
leggere
to read

Io ______ **il libro.**

Lui / Lei ______ **il giornale.**

Noi leggiamo/ **la lista.**

Lei ______ **molto.**

Loro ______ **tutto.**

Può *(pwah)* (can) **Lei** translate these thoughts **sotto in italiano? Le risposte sono sotto.**

1. I can speak Italian. ______
2. He must pay now. ______
3. We don't know the address. ______
4. You owe us 10,000 lire. Lei ci deve dieci mila lire.
5. She knows everything. ______
6. I am able to speak Italian. ______

RISPOSTE

1. Posso parlare italiano.
2. Deve pagare adesso.
3. Non sappiamo l'indirizzo.
4. Lei ci deve dieci mila lire.
5. Sa tutto.
6. Posso parlare l'italiano.

Adesso, draw **delle linee** *(lee-neh)* **fra** the opposites **sotto.** Don't forget to say them out loud. Use **queste** *(kweh-steh)* (these) **parole** every day to describe **le cose nella Sua** *(soo-ah)* (your) **casa, nella Sua scuola,** *(skoo-oh-lah)* (school) at work, etc.

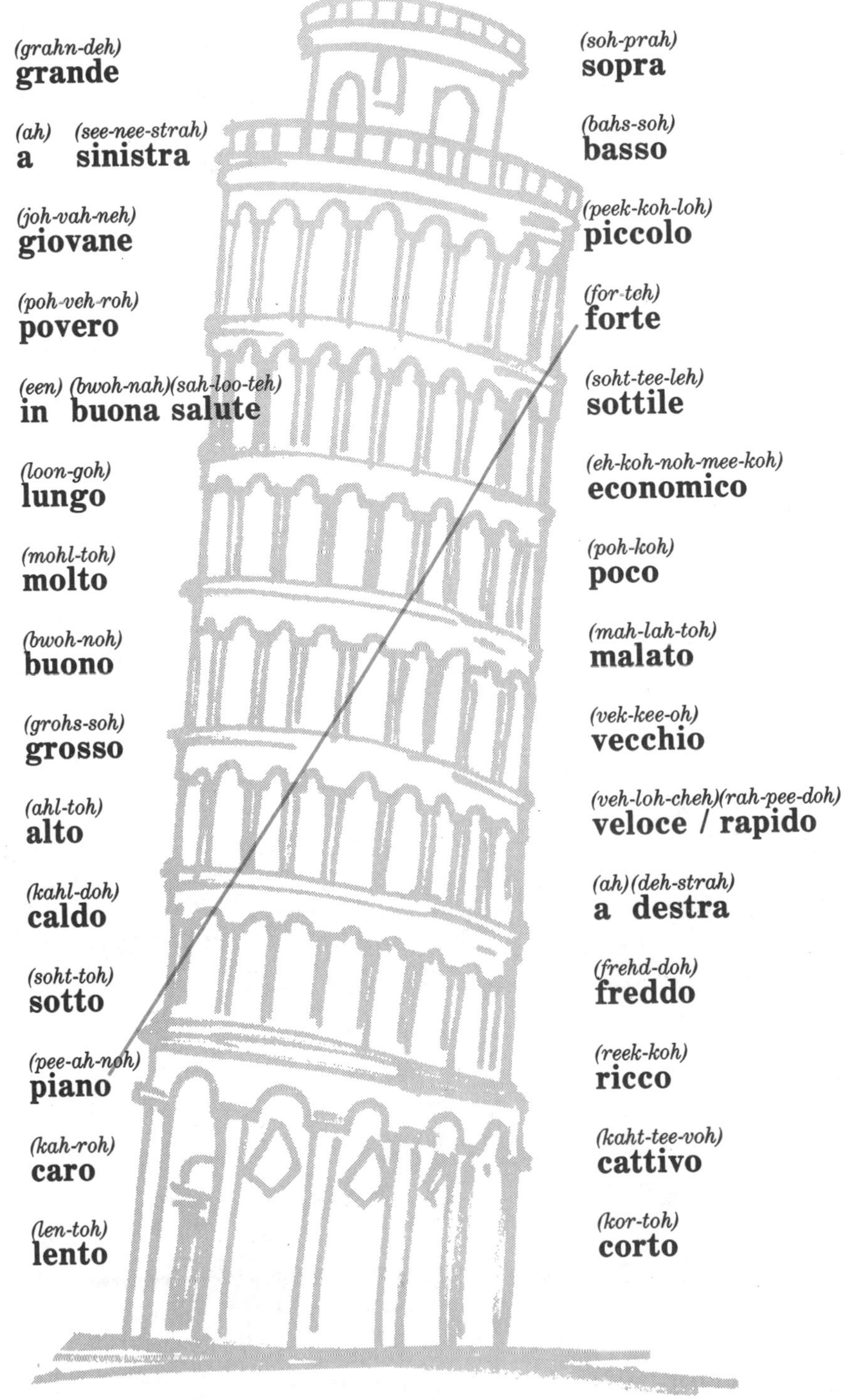

- ☐ **straordinario** *(strah-ohr-dee-nah-ree-oh)* . . . extraordinary ______
- ☐ **lo studio** *(stoo-dee-oh)* . . . . study, studio ______
- ☐ **il successo** *(soo-chehs-soh)* . . . . success ______
- ☐ **sud** *(sood)* . . . . south ______
- ☐ **superiore** *(soo-peh-ree-oh-reh)* . . . . superior, above ______

Step 17

Il Viaggiatore *(vee-ah-jah-toh-reh)* [traveler] Viaggia *(vee-ah-jah)* [travels]

Ieri a Venezia! **Oggi a Milano!** **Domani a Bologna!**

Lunedì a Firenze! **Mercoledì a Napoli!** **Venerdì a Brindisi!**

Traveling è easy and quite efficient **in Italia. L'Italia non è grande,** therefore **il viaggio è molto facile** *(fah-chee-leh)* [easy] within the distinctive "boot" **che** *(keh)* [that] **si** *(see)* [is] **chiama** *(kee-ah-mah)* [called] **"l'Italia."**

Come viaggiare *(vee-ah-jah-reh)* [travel] **in Italia?**

Stefano viaggia in macchina.

Franca viaggia in treno.

Francesca viaggia in aereo.

Anna viaggia in nave *(nah-veh)* [ship]**.**

Andrea e Silvia viaggiano in bicicletta attraverso *(aht-trah-vehr-soh)* [across] **l'Italia.**

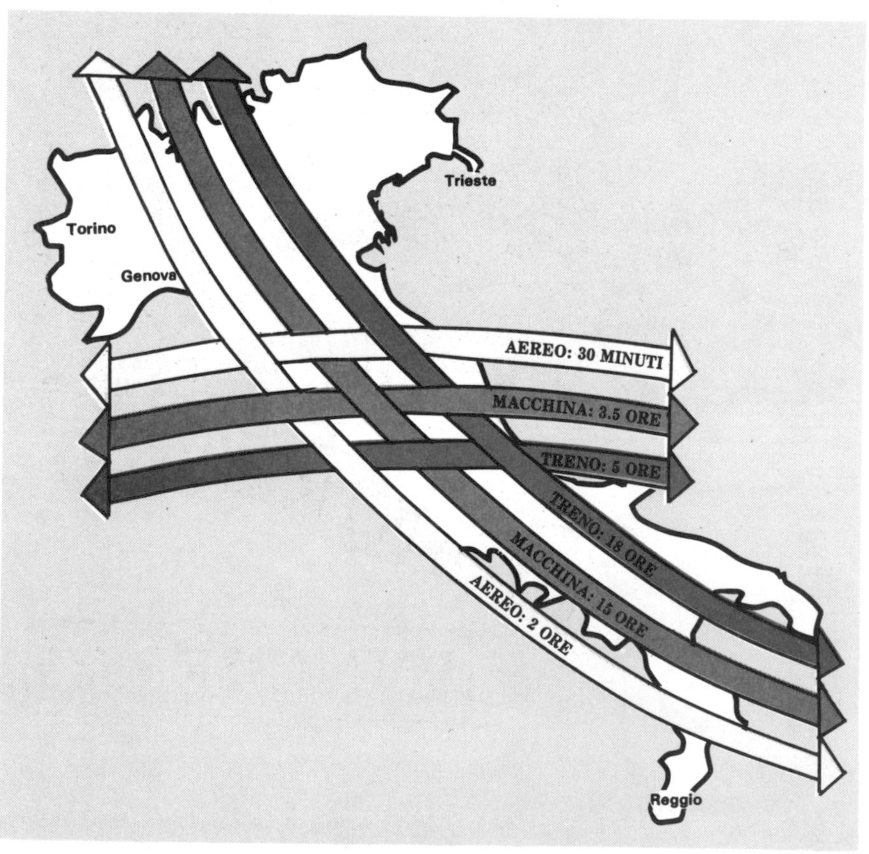

Guardi *(goo-ahr-dee)* [look at] **la carta geografica a sinistra.**

È l'Italia, non è vero? [isn't it]

Per viaggiare dal nord al sud in aereo, ci *(chee)* [it] **vogliono** *(vohl-yah-noh)* [takes] **solamente due ore, 15 ore in macchina, 18 ore in treno. Non c'è** *(cheh)* **male, vero?** [not bad, is it]

- ☐ **il tabacco** *(tah-bahk-koh)* . . . . tobacco
- ☐ **il tassì** *(tahs-see)* . . . . taxi
- ☐ **il tavolo** *(tah-voh-loh)* . . . . table
  - **—la tavola calda** . . . . cafeteria
- ☐ **il teatro** *(teh-ah-troh)* . . . . theater

Gli Italiani enjoy going on **vacanze,** *(vah-kahn-tseh)* vacation, so it is no **sorpresa** *(sohr-preh-sah)* surprise, to find **molte parole** built on **la parola "viaggiare,"** *(vee-ah-jah-reh)* which means "to travel." Practice saying **le parole seguenti** many times. **Lei** will use them **spesso.** *(spehs-soh)* often

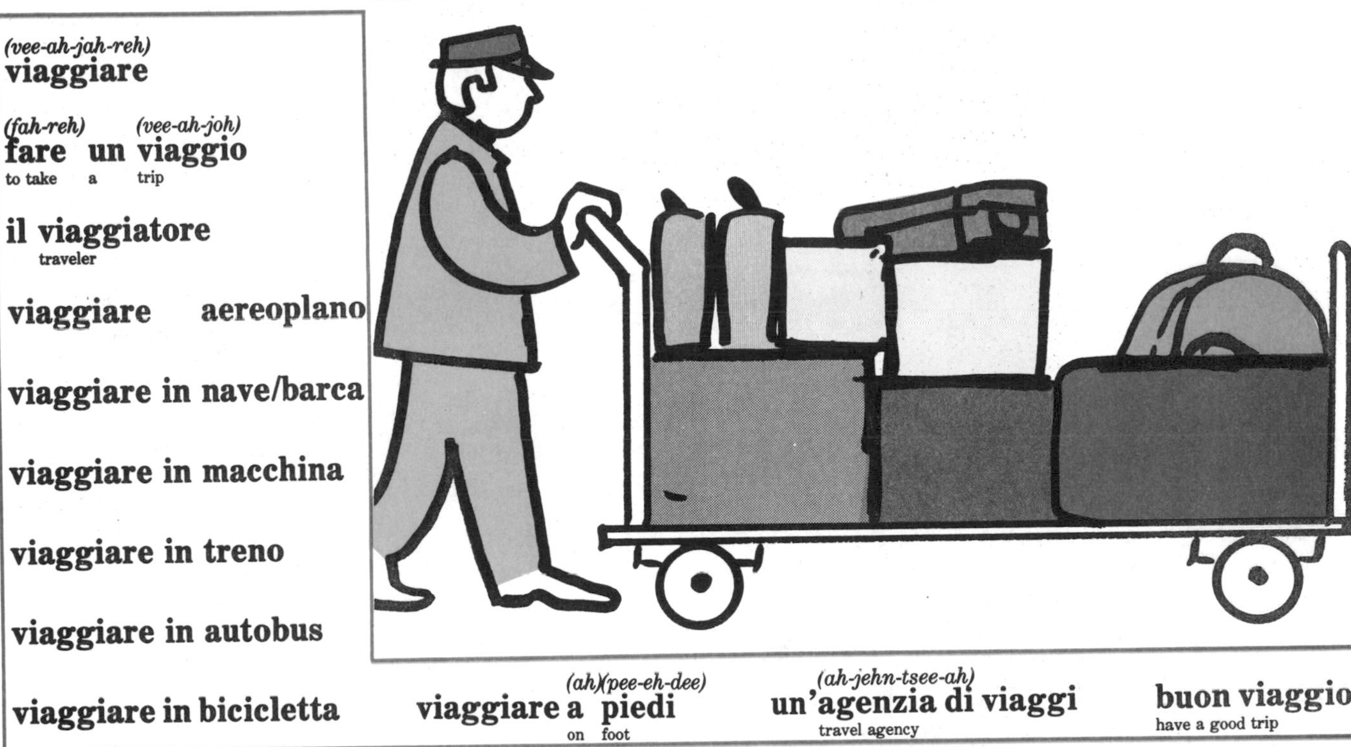

viaggiare *(vee-ah-jah-reh)*

fare un viaggio *(fah-reh) (vee-ah-joh)* — to take a trip

il viaggiatore — traveler

viaggiare aereoplano

viaggiare in nave/barca

viaggiare in macchina

viaggiare in treno

viaggiare in autobus

viaggiare in bicicletta

viaggiare a piedi *(ah)(pee-eh-dee)* — on foot

un'agenzia di viaggi *(ah-jehn-tsee-ah)* — travel agency

buon viaggio! — have a good trip

Sotto ci sono *(chee)* some basic signs which **Lei deve** *(deh-veh)* should also learn to recognize quickly. Most of **queste parole** *(kwes-teh)* come from **i verbi** **entrare** *(en-trah-reh)* = to go in/enter **e** **uscire** *(oos-chee-reh)* = to go out.

L'USCITA

L'ENTRATA

L'INGRESSO

l'entrata *(len-trah-tah)* entrance or **l'ingresso** *(leen-gres-soh)* entrance ______________

l'entrata principale *(preen-chee-pah-leh)* main entrance ______________

l'entrata laterale *(lah-teh-rah-leh)* side entrance ______________

l'uscita *(loo-shee-tah)* exit — *l'uscita* ______________

l'uscita principale main exit ______________

l'uscita di sicurezza *(see-koo-reh-tsah)* emergency exit ______________

vietato l'ingresso *(vee-eh-tah-toh)* do not enter ______________

- ☐ **il telefono** *(teh-leh-foh-noh)* .... telephone ______________
- ☐ **il telegramma** *(teh-leh-grahm-mah)* .... telegram ______________
- ☐ **il televisore** *(teh-leh-vee-soh-reh)* .... television set ______________
- ☐ **la temperatura** *(tem-peh-rah-too-rah)* ...... temperature ______________
- ☐ **il Tevere** *(teh-veh-reh)* .... Tiber River ______________

(ahn-dah-reh) *(vee-ah-jah-toh-reh)*
Andare **è un verbo molto importante per il viaggiatore.** If you choose to **andare in macchina,** here are a few key **parole.**
to go — traveler

(lah-oo-toh-strah-dah)
l'autostrada l'autostrada
highway

(kohn-trahv-ven-tsee-oh-neh) *(mool-tah)*
una contravvenzione or **una multa** ____________
traffic ticket — traffic fine

(strah-dah)
la strada per Verona ____________
road to Verona

(mahk-kee-nah) *(noh-leh-jah-reh)*
una macchina da noleggiare ____________
rental car

(ah-jehn-tsee-ah) *(noh-leh-joh)*
un'agenzia di noleggio ____________
car rental agency

Ecco quattro opposites **molto importanti.**

Milano-**Bologna-Prato-Firenze**-Roma

Km Dist.		R33 rapido 1 e 2	17 1 e 2	23 1 e 2	MS 1 e 2	1475 accel. 1 e 2	65 1 e 2	49 1 e 2	R496 rapido autom. 1 cl.
		TRENO AZZURRO Carrozza Pullmann Milano-Napoli	HOLLAND-ITALIEN EXPRESS SKANDINAVIEN-ITALIEN EXPRESS		FRECCIA DEL SUD		ALPEN EXPRESS		
	Milano C. . . . . p.	1300	1305	1350	1450	...	1540	...	...
	Bologna C. . . . . a.	1513	1543	1639	1718	...	1806	...	...
»	**Bologna C.** . p.	1518	1551	1704	1738	1800	1822	1902	1921
7	Bologna S. Ruffillo .					1810			
17	Pianoro					1821			
26	Monzuno-Vado . .					1831			
36	Grizzana					1842			
41	S. Ben. S. -Cast. Pep.					1859			
61	Vernio -Mont.-Cant.					1917			
71	Vaiano					1927			
81	**Prato** 232, 251 a.			1805		1938	1924	2003	
	p.			1807		1940	1925	2004	
85	Calenzano					—			
89	Sesto Fiorentino . .					1948			
93	Castello					—			
95	Firenze Rifredi a.					—			
97	**Firenze** S.M.N. 231 a.	1624	1702	1825	1857	1955	1937	2017	2023
	Firenze S.M.N. p.	1632	1712	1839	1909	...	1949	...	...
	Roma Termini . a.	2005	2055	2310	2245	...	2333	...	...

(lah-ree-voh)
l'arrivo ____________
arrival

(pahr-ten-tsah)
la partenza la partenza
departure

(een-tair-nah-tsee-oh-nahl-ee)
internazionale ____________
international

(nah-tsee-oh-nahl-ee)
nazionale ____________
domestic

(vee-ah-joh)
Let's learn the basic **verbi di viaggio.** Follow the same pattern you have in previous Steps.

(vee-ah-jah-reh)
viaggiare = to travel
____

(aht-tehr-rah-reh)
atterrare = to land
atterrare

(preh-noh-tah-reh)
prenotare = to reserve/to book
____

(ahr-ree-vah-reh)
arrivare = to arrive
____

(pahr-tee-reh)
partire = to leave
____

(gwee-dah-reh)
guidare = to drive (cars)
____

(sah-lee-reh)
salire = to board/ to climb into
____

(shen-deh-reh)
scendere = to get out/ go down
____

(kahm-bee-ah-reh)
cambiare (treno) = to transfer (trains)
____

(ahn-dah-reh) *(ah-air-ee-oh)*
andare in aereo = to go by plane/fly
____

- ☐ **il terrazzo** *(tehr-rah-tsoh)* . . . . terrace ____________
- ☐ **il tesoro** *(teh-soh-roh)* . . . . treasure ____________
- ☐ **il titolo** *(tee-toh-loh)* . . . . title ____________
- ☐ **la torre** *(tohr-reh)* . . . . tower ____________
  —La Torre Pendente . . . . Leaning Tower (of Pisa) ____________

(vee-ah-joh)

Con questi verbi, Lei è ready for any **viaggio** anywhere. **Lei** should have no **problemi con i verbi.** Just remember the basic "plug-in" formula **noi** learned already. Use that knowledge to translate the following thoughts **in italiano. Le risposte sono sotto.**

1. I fly (go by plane) to Rome. ______________________
2. I transfer trains in Milan. ______________________
3. He lands in Paris. ______________________
4. We arrive tomorrow. ______________________
5. You get out in Florence. ______________________
6. They travel to Rome. ______________________
7. Where is the train to Padua? ______________________
8. How can one fly (go by plane) to Switzerland? With Swissair or Alitalia? ______________________

____

Ecco *(ahl-koo-neh)* **alcune** (some) **parole nuove per il** *(soo-oh)* **Suo** (your) **viaggio.** As always, write out **le parole e** practice the sample *(frah-see)* **frasi** (sentences) out loud.

(mahr-chah-pee-eh-deh) **il marciapiede** (platform) **e il** *(bee-nah-ree-oh)* **binario** (train track)

____

Mi scusi. Dov'è il binario numero due?

(stah-tsee-oh-neh) **la stazione dei treni** (train station)

____

Mi scusi. Dov'è la stazione dei treni?

(lah-air-ee-oh-pohr-toh) **l'aereoporto** (airport)

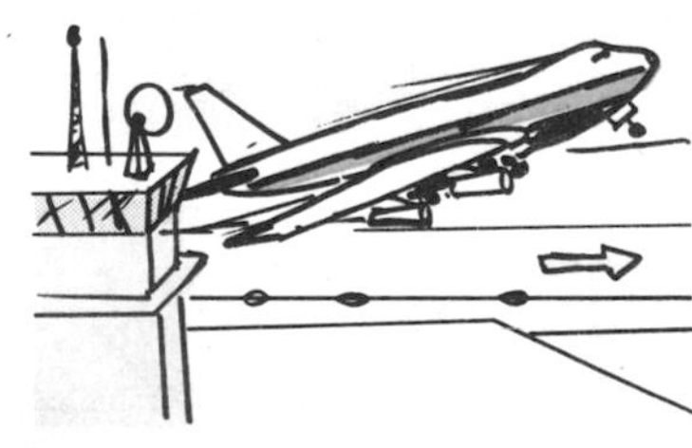

l'aereoporto

Mi scusi. Dov'è l'aereoporto?

RISPOSTE

1. **Vado in aereo a Roma.**
2. **Cambio treno a Milano.**
3. **Atterra a Parigi.**
4. **Arriviamo domani.**
5. **Scende a Firenze.**
6. **Viaggiano a Roma.**
7. **Dov'è il treno per Padova?**
8. **Come si può andare in aereo in Svizzera? Con Swissair o con Alitalia?**

(loof-fee-choh) *(kahm-bee-oh)*
l'ufficio di cambio
money-exchange office

____

Mi scusi. Dov'è l'ufficio di cambio?

(oh-jet-tee) *(smah-ree-tee)*
l'ufficio oggetti smarriti
lost-and-found office

____

Mi scusi. Dov'è l'ufficio oggetti smarriti?

(loh-rah-ree-oh) *(fehr-roh-vee-eh)*
l'orario delle ferrovie
timetable railroad

____

Mi scusi. Dov'è l'orario?

(ohk-koo-pah-toh)
occupato ____________________
occupied

(lee-beh-roh)
libero ____________________
free

(skohm-pahr-tee-men-toh)
lo scompartimento ____________________
compartment

(poh-stoh)
il posto *il posto*
seat

(kweh-stoh)
Questo posto è occupato? ____________________
this is

Questo posto è libero? ____________________

(skohm-pahr-tee-men-toh)
Questo scompartimento è occupato? ____________________

Questo scompartimento è libero? ____________________

Practice writing out **le domande seguenti.** It will help you *(pee-oo)(tahr-dee)* **più tardi.** (later)

Mi scusi. Dove sono i gabinetti? ____________________

Mi scusi. Dov'è il *(vah-goh-neh)(ree-stoh-rahn-teh)* **vagone ristorante?** ____________________
dining car

Dov'è la *(sah-lah) (dah-spet-toh)* **sala d'aspetto?** *Dov'è la sala d'aspetto?*
waiting room

Dov'è lo *(spohr-tel-loh)* **sportello numero otto?** ____________________

(vee-eh-tah-toh)(foo-mah-reh)
È vietato fumare? ____________________
is it prohibited to smoke

- ☐ **il tram** *(trahm)* .... tram, street car ____________
- ☐ **tranquillo** *(trahn-kweel-loh)* .... calm, tranquil ____________
- ☐ **tre** *(treh)* .... three ____________
- ☐ **il treno** *(treh-noh)* .... train ____________
- ☐ **il turista** *(too-ree-stah)* .... tourist ____________

Increase your **parole di** *(vee-ah-joh)* **viaggio** by writing out **le parole sotto e** practicing the *(frah-see)* **frasi** (sentences) out loud.

(pehr) **per** (for/to) ______________________
Dov'è il treno per Roma?

(tem-poh) **tempo** (time) ______________________
Ho molto poco tempo.

il *(bee-nah-ree-oh)* **binario** (track) ______________________
Il treno parte dal binario numero tre.

l'ufficio *(een-for-mah-tsee-oh-see)* **informazioni** (information office) ______________________

l'ufficio *(deh-poh-see-toh)* **deposito** *(bah-gahl-yee)* **bagagli** (left-luggage office) ______________________
____
Dov'è l'ufficio deposito bagagli?

il *(fahk-kee-noh)* **facchino** (porter) ______________________

il *(beel-yet-toh)* **biglietto** (airplane/train ticket) il biglietto

Practice **queste parole** every day. **Lei** will be surprised how *(spehs-soh)* **spesso** (often) **Lei** will use them.

(poo-oh) **Può** (can) **Lei leggere la lezione seguente?**

Lei è adesso *(seh-doo-toh)* **seduto** (seated) **nell'aereoplano e va in Italia. Lei ha** exchanged **il denaro** (you have, haven't you?). **Lei ha i biglietti e il** *(pahs-sah-pohr-toh)* **passaporto e ha i** *(bah-gahl-yee)* **bagagli** (bags/suitcases) all packed. **Adesso, è un turista. Lei** *(aht-tehr-rah)* **atterra domani alle 14,15 in Italia. Buon viaggio! Buon divertimento!**

Adesso, Lei have arrived **e Lei** head for **la stazione** in order to get to **la Sua** *(deh-stee-nah-tsee-oh-neh)* **destinazione** (destination) *(fee-nah-leh)* **finale.** As **Lei** know, **i treni italiani** come in varying speeds: **il** *(rah-pee-doh)* **rapido e l'espresso (molto rapidi); il** *(dee-ret-toh)* **diretto e il** *(dee-ret-tees-see-moh)* **direttissimo (rapidi); e** *(lah-cheh-leh-rah-toh)* **l'accelerato (lento).** Some **treni** *(ahn-noh)* **hanno** (have) **il** *(vah-goh-neh)* **vagone** (dining car) *(ree-stoh-rahn-teh)* **ristorante e** some **treni hanno il vagone** *(let-toh)* **letto** (sleeping car) **o le** *(koo-chet-teh)* **cuccette** (berths).

All this will be indicated **sull'orario,** but remember **Lei sa come** to ask things like this.

Practice your possible *(kohm-bee-nah-tsee-oh-nee)* **combinazioni** (combinations) **di domande** by writing out the following samples.

(cheh) **C'è** (is there) **un vagone ristorante sul treno?** ______________________

(chee) **Ci sono delle** *(koo-chet-teh)* **cuccette sul treno?** ______________________

C'è un vagone letto sul treno? ______________________

- ☐ **l'ufficio** *(loof-fee-choh)* . . . . office ______________
- ☐ **ultimo** *(ool-tee-moh)* . . . . final, last, ultimate ______________
- ☐ **unico** *(oo-nee-koh)* . . . . unique, only, single ______________
- **—senso unico** . . . . one-way (traffic sign) ______________
- ☐ **universale** *(oo-nee-vehr-sah-leh)* . . . . universal ______________

What about inquiring about **il prezzo** *(preh-tsoh)* price **dei biglietti** *(beel-yet-tee)* **o la tariffa?** *(tah-reef-fah)* fare **Lei può fare** *(fah-reh)* make **delle** some **domande.**

Quanto *(kwahn-toh)* **è il biglietto (la tariffa) per Taranto?** ____________________

semplice *(sem-plee-cheh)* one-way ____________________ **andata e ritorno** *(ahn-dah-tah) (ree-tohr-noh)* round-trip ____________________

Quanto è il biglietto per Siena? *(see-eh-nah)* ____________________

Quanto è il biglietto per Bari? *(bah-ree)* ____________________

Semplice *(sem-plee-cheh)* **o andata e ritorno?** ____________________

What about times of **partenze** *(pahr-ten-tseh)* departures **e arrivi?** *(ahr-ree-vee)* arrivals **Lei può fare queste domande anche.**

A che ora parte leaves **il treno per Belluno?** ____________________

A che ora parte l'aereoplano per Roma? ____________________

A che ora arriva il treno da from **Parigi?** *(pah-ree-jee)* ____________________

A che ora arriva il volo *(voh-loh)* flight **da Nuova York?** ____________________

Lei have arrived **in Italia. Lei è adesso alla stazione. Dove vorrebbe** *(vohr-rehb-beh)* would you like **andare?** Well, tell that to **la persona** at the **sportello** selling **i biglietti.** *(beel-yet-tee)*

Vorrei andare in Francia. *(frahn-chah)* ____________________

Vorrei andare a Rimini. *(ree-mee-nee)* ____________________

Vorremmo andare a Ravenna. *(rah-ven-nah)* ____________________

A che ora parte il treno per Napoli? *(nah-poh-lee)* ____________________

Quanto costa il biglietto per Catanzaro? *(kah-tahn-zah-roh)* ____________________

Vorrei un biglietto per Lecce. *(leh-cheh)* ____________________

prima *(pree-mah)* first **classe** *(klahs-seh)* class ____________________ **seconda** *(seh-kohn-dah)* second **classe** class ____________________

Semplice o andata e ritorno? ____________________

Devo *(deh-voh)* must I **cambiare treno?** ____________________ **Grazie.** ____________________

Con this practice, **Lei è** off **e** running. **Queste parole di viaggio** will make your holiday twice as enjoyable **e** at least three times as easy. Review **queste parole nuove** by doing the crossword puzzle **alla pagina** 77. Practice drilling yourself on this Step by selecting other locations e asking your own **domande** about **i treni, gli** *(l-yee)* **autobus o gli aereoplani** that go there. Select **parole nuove dal Suo** *(soo-oh)* (your) **dizionario e** practice asking questions that **cominciano** *(koh-meen-chah-noh)* (begin) **con**

DOVE	**QUANDO**	**QUANTO**	**QUANTE VOLTE** *(vohl-teh)* how often/how many times

o making statements like

Vorrei andare a Roma.

Vorrei comprare un biglietto.

PAROLE CROCIATE *(kroh-chah-teh)*

ACROSS

1. lease/rent
2. have a good trip
3. to smoke
4. occupied
5. timetable
6. money
7. foreign
8. flight
9. nothing
10. time
11. to board/to climb into
12. to leave
13. arrival
14. entrance
15. station
16. to reserve
17. to get out/go down
18. domestic

DOWN

1. we/us
2. to drive
3. information office
4. prohibited
5. track
6. exit
7. train
8. to fly/go by plane
9. ticket window
10. free
11. traveler
12. passport
13. departure

RISPOSTE ALLE PAROLE CROCIATE *(kroh-chah-teh)*

ACROSS

1. noleggio
2. buon viaggio
3. fumare
4. occupato
5. orario
6. denaro
7. straniero
8. volo
9. niente
10. tempo
11. salire
12. partire
13. arrivo
14. entrata
15. stazione
16. prenotare
17. scendere
18. domestico

DOWN

1. noi
2. guidare
3. ufficio informazioni
4. vietato
5. binario
6. uscita
7. treno
8. volare
9. sportello
10. libero
11. viaggiatore
12. passaporto
13. partenza

Step 18

Lei è adesso in Italia e Lei ha una camera. E adesso? Lei ha (have) fame (fah-meh) (hunger). Vorrebbe (you would like) mangiare (mahn-jah-reh). **Ma** (mah) (but), **dov'è un buon ristorante?** First of all, **ci** (chee) **sono** different types of places to eat. Let's learn them.

il ristorante (ree-stoh-rahn-teh)	= exactly what it says, with a variety of meals and prices
la trattoria (traht-toh-ree-ah)	= usually less elegant and less expensive than a **ristorante,** often run by a family
l'osteria (loh-steh-ree-ah)	= found in the country or in small towns, serves mostly drinks and easy-to-prepare food
la tavola calda (tah-voh-lah)(kahl-dah)	= similar to a cafeteria, serving a variety of foods (You may eat sitting down or standing up.)
il bar (bahr)	= serves pastries and sandwiches, concentrates on liquid refreshments (great place for morning coffee or tea)

Try them all. Experiment. **Adesso Lei trova un buon ristorante. Entra nel ristorante e trova un posto** (seat). Sharing **tavole con** others **è** a common **e molto** pleasant **costume** (koh-stoo-meh) (custom) **in Europa.** If **Lei vede** (veh-deh) (see) **una sedia** vacant, just be sure to ask

Mi scusi. Questo posto è libero (lee-beh-roh)**?**

If **Lei ha bisogno** (need) **di una lista,** catch the attention of **il cameriere** (kah-meh-ree-eh-reh) **e** say

Cameriere! La lista, per favore.

- ☐ **l'università** *(loo-nee-vehr-see-tah)*....... university
- ☐ **urbano** *(oor-bah-noh)*................. urban
- ☐ **usato** *(oo-sah-toh)*.................. used, second-hand
- ☐ **usuale** *(oo-soo-ah-leh)*................ usual, customary
- ☐ **l'utensile** *(loo-ten-see-leh)*............ utensil

In Italia, ci sono tre main **pasti** *(pah-stee)* meals to enjoy every day, plus **un caffè** *(kahf-feh)* **e** perhaps **un dolce** *(dohl-cheh)* pastry **per il viaggiatore** *(vee-ah-jah-toh-reh)* traveler **stanco** *(stahn-koh)* tired late in **il pomeriggio.** *(poh-meh-ree-joh)*

la colazione *(koh-lah-tsee-oh-neh)* or **la prima colazione**	=	breakfast . . . This is a "continental breakfast" with **caffè o tè e pane** or a sweet roll. Be sure to check serving times before retiring.
il pranzo *(prahn-zoh)*	=	lunch. . . . . . This is the big meal of the day. It usually includes a pasta dish or soup, an entree and salad. It is generally served from noon to 14:00.
la cena *(cheh-nah)*	=	dinner. . . . . This is a light meal often consisting of soup, cheese or eggs. It is generally served from 19:30 to 22:00.

If **Lei** look around you **nel ristorante italiano, Lei** will see that some **costumi** *(koh-stoo-mee)* customs **italiani sono differenti** *(deef-feh-ren-tee)* from ours. **Il pane** *(pah-neh)* may be set directly on the tablecloth, elbows are often rested **sulla tavola** and please do not forget to mop up your **sugo** *(soo-goh)* sauce **con il Suo pane! Lei** will hear **"Buon appetito!"** *(bwohn) (ahp-peh-tee-toh)* before **il Suo pasto e** an inquiring **"Ha mangiato bene?"** *(ah) (mahn-jah-toh) (beh-neh)* did you eat well after **Lei** have finished. **Il cameriere** is asking if **Lei** enjoyed **il Suo pasto e** if it tasted good. A smile **e** a **"Sí, grazie"** will tell him that you enjoyed it.

Adesso, it may be **prima colazione** *(koh-lah-tsee-oh-neh)* time **a Denver, ma** but **Lei è in Italia e sono le 19,00.** Many **ristoranti italiani** post **la lista** outside. Always read it before entering so **Lei sa** what type of **pasto e prezzo** *(preh-tsoh)* price **Lei** will encounter inside. Most **ristoranti** offer **il piatto del giorno** *(pee-aht-toh) (johr-noh)* special meal of the day **o una lista a prezzo fisso.** *(preh-tsoh)* fixed These are complete **pasti** at fair **prezzi.** In addition, **ci sono** all the following main categories **sulla lista.**

- ☐ **le vacanze** *(vah-kahn-tseh)* . . . . vacation __________
  - **—fare le vacanze** . . . . to go on vacation __________
- ☐ **la vaccinazione** *(vah-chee-nah-tsee-oh-neh)* . . vaccination __________
- ☐ **la vaniglia** *(vah-neel-yah)* . . . . vanilla __________
- ☐ **il vaporetto** *(vah-poh-ret-toh)*. . . . . steam ferry (many in Venice) __________

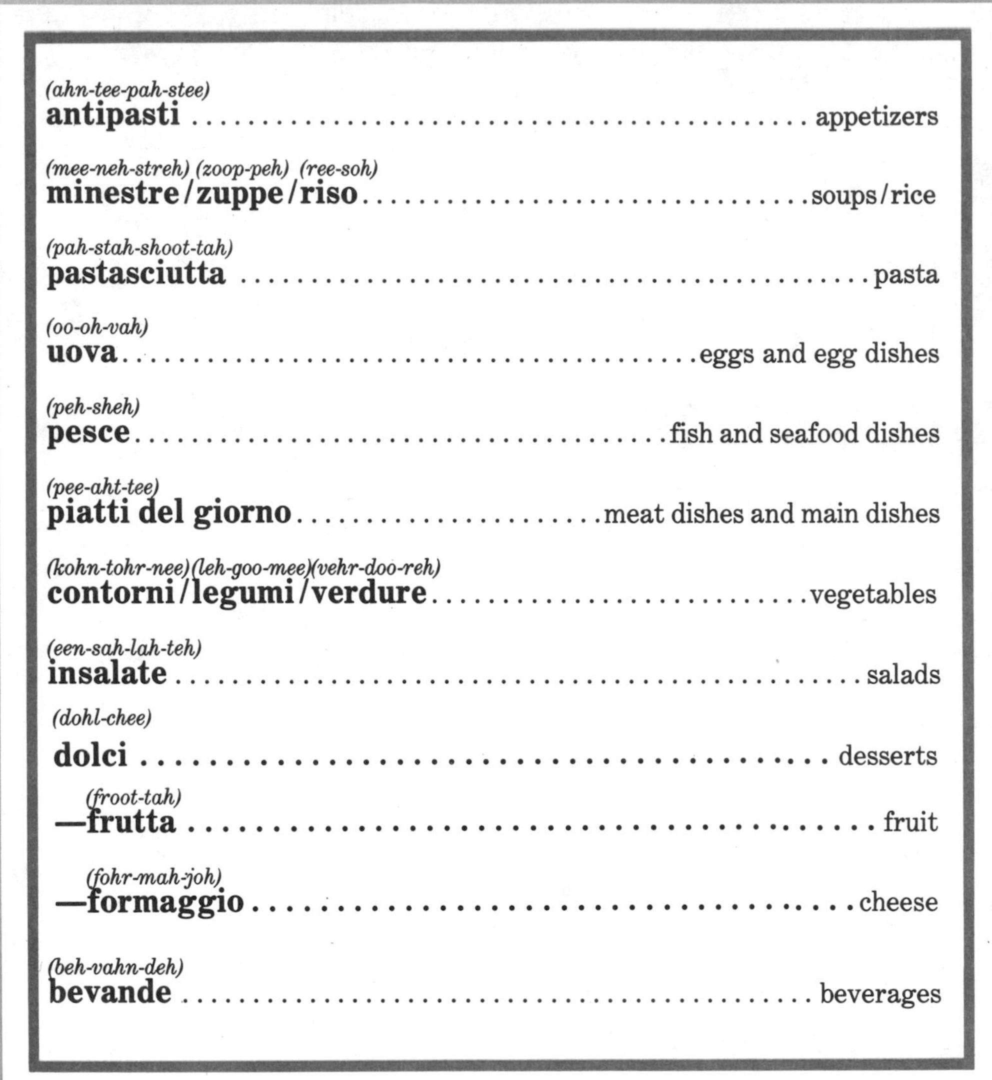

(ahn-tee-pah-stee)
antipasti .... appetizers

(mee-neh-streh) (zoop-peh) (ree-soh)
minestre / zuppe / riso .... soups / rice

(pah-stah-shoot-tah)
pastasciutta .... pasta

(oo-oh-vah)
uova .... eggs and egg dishes

(peh-sheh)
pesce .... fish and seafood dishes

(pee-aht-tee)
piatti del giorno .... meat dishes and main dishes

(kohn-tohr-nee) (leh-goo-mee) (vehr-doo-reh)
contorni / legumi / verdure .... vegetables

(een-sah-lah-teh)
insalate .... salads

(dohl-chee)
dolci .... desserts

(froot-tah)
—frutta .... fruit

(fohr-mah-joh)
—formaggio .... cheese

(beh-vahn-deh)
bevande .... beverages

Most **ristoranti** also offer **le specialità** *(speh-chah-lee-tah)* (specialties) **della casa o** special meals prepared **dal cuoco** *(koo-oh-koh)* (cook). And if **Lei** are sampling **il vino,** don't forget to ask about the **vino della casa** (house wine). **Adesso** for a preview of delights to come . . . At the back of this **libro, Lei trova** a sample **lista italiana. Legga la lista oggi** *(oh-jee)* **e impari le parole nuove! Quando Lei** are ready to leave for **Europa,** cut out **la lista,** fold it **e** carry it in your pocket, wallet **o** purse. **Lei può** *(poo-oh)* (can) **andare in** any **ristorante e** feel prepared. (May we suggest studying **la lista** after, **e** not before, **Lei ha** eaten!)

- ☐ **la varietà** *(vah-ree-eh-tah)* .... variety ______
- ☐ **il vaso** *(vah-soh)* .... vase ______
- ☐ **la vena** *(veh-nah)* .... vein ______
- ☐ **il venditore** *(vehn-dee-toh-reh)* .... vendor, seller ______
- ☐ **la versione** *(vehr-see-oh-neh)* .... version ______

In addition, learning the following should help **Lei** to identify what kind of meat **o** poultry **Lei ordina** (order) **e come** (how) it will be prepared.

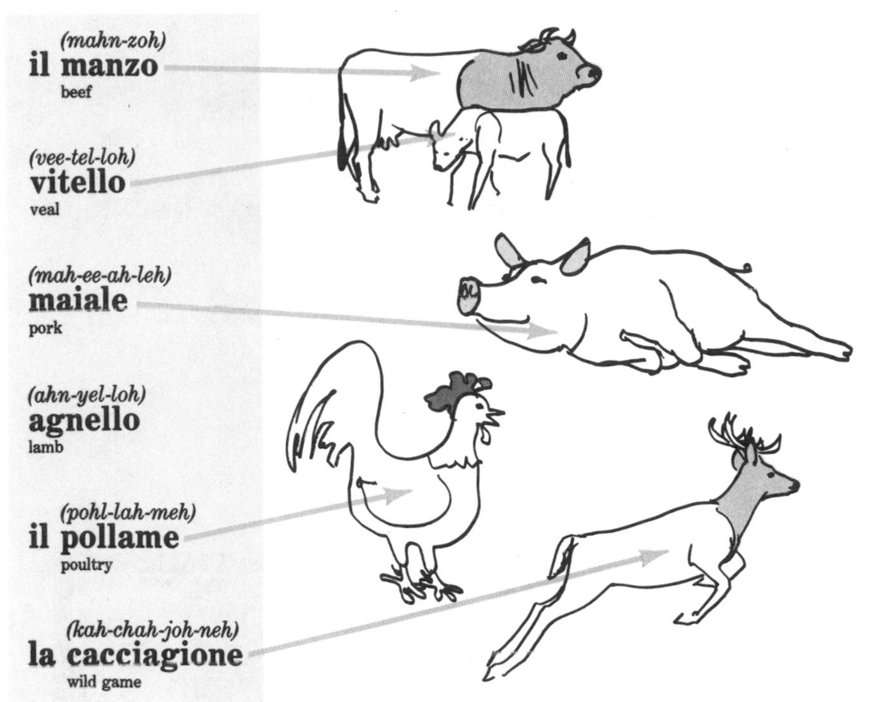

(koht-toh)
cotto = cooked

(ahr-roh-stoh)
arrosto = roasted

(freet-toh)
fritto = fried

(ahl) (fohr-noh)
al forno = baked

(greel-yah)
alla griglia = grilled

(fahr-chee-toh)
farcito = stuffed

Lei will also get **verdure** *(vehr-doo-reh)* (vegetables) **con il Suo pasto** and perhaps **un'insalata verde** *(vehr-deh)* (green)**.** One day at an open-air **mercato** *(mehr-kah-toh)* (market) will teach you **i nomi** for all the different kinds of **verdure e frutta** *(froot-tah)***,** plus it will be a delightful experience for you. **Lei può** (can) always consult your menu guide at the back of **questo libro** if **Lei dimentica** *(dee-men-tee-kah)* (forget) **il nome corretto. Adesso Lei ha** decided what **Lei vorrebbe** *(vor-rehb-beh)* **mangiare e il cameriere arriva.**

☐ **la vergine** *(vehr-jee-neh)*	virgin	______
—la Santa Vergine	Holy Virgin	______
☐ **la via** *(vee-ah)*; **via**	way; by	______
—via Appia Antica	Appian Way	______
—via aerea	by air, airmail	______

(see) (dee-men-tee-kee) (dohl-cheh)
Non si dimentichi to treat yourself to **un dolce italiano. Lei** would not want to miss out on
don't forget

trying **i dolci seguenti.**

(krehm) **una crème caramel** custard with burnt sugar sauce	(kahn-noh-lee) **cannoli** pastries filled with sweetened ricotta cheese
(grah-nee-tah) **granita** ice with fruit syrup or coffee	(zah-bahl-yoh-neh) **zabaglione** custard of eggs, sugar and wine

After completing **il Suo pasto,** call **il cameriere e** pay just as **Lei ha** already learned in Step 16:

Cameriere, vorrei il conto, per favore.

(cheh)
Sotto c'è una sample **lista** to help you prepare for your holiday.

TRATTORIA TRE FONTANE

LA LISTA

ANTIPASTI

Antipasti assortiti (assorted appetizers)	£700
Prosciutto crudo di Parma (raw-cured ham)	700
Insalata russa (cooked vegetables and hard-boiled eggs, mixed with mayonnaise)	600
Insalata di pesce (seafood salad)	850

MINESTRE E PASTA

Tortellini in brodo (stuffed pasta in broth)	450
Zuppa di vongole (clam chowder)	350
Zuppa pavese (egg soup)	400
Lasagne a forno (meat, cheese and pasta casserole)	450
Ravioli alla romagnola (pasta stuffed with cheeses)	400
Spaghetti di carne (pasta covered in meat sauce)	350

PESCE

Fritto misto di mare (floured and deep-fried seafood)	1000
Calamaretti fritti (breaded and deep-fried gray mullet)	1000
Sogliola alla Margherita (poached sole covered with Hollandaise sauce)	1500
Cozze alla livornese (mussels in tomato sauce on toast)	850
Spiedino mare (broiled pieces of marinated seafood)	1200

PIATTI DEL GIORNO

Costoletta alla milanese (breaded, unboned veal steak)	850
Abbacchio alla romana (roasted milk-fed lamb)	1200
Vitello tonnato (cold veal cutlets covered in sauce)	1350
Bistecca alla fiorentina (broiled unboned rib steak)	1450
Saltimbocca alla romana (fried slices of veal and ham)	1600
Pollo alla cacciatore (chicken braised in onions, herbs and wine)	1000
Trippe alla bolognese (broiled beef tripe)	800

CONTORNI

Asparagi alla parmigiana (boiled asparagus with Parmesan)	300
Patate fritte (French-fried potatoes)	300
Insalata mista (mixed salad)	300
Insalata verde (green salad)	300
Zucchini trifolati (zucchini cooked in butter and garlic)	400

FORMAGGI

Assortiti a porzione (assorted cheeses)	500

DOLCI

Frutta di stagione, un pezzo (seasonal fruit)	300
St. Honoré (custard pastry and cream puffs dipped in syrup)	500
Cassata alla siciliana (sponge cake layered with sweetened Ricotta cheese, chocolate and fruit)	450
Macedonia di frutta (fruit salad)	450

BEVANDE

Vino (bicchiere)	300
Vino (litro)	1300
Birra	300
Acqua minerale (mineral water)	100
Limonata	150
Succo di frutta (fruit juice)	250
Latte	200
Caffè	150
Tè	150

☐ **vigoroso** *(vee-goh-roh-soh)* . . . . vigorous ________
☐ **il vino** *(vee-noh)* . . . . wine ________
☐ **la visita** *(vee-see-tah)* . . . . visit ________
—fare una visita . . . . to pay a visit ________
☐ **la vitamina** *(vee-tah-mee-nah)* . . . . vitamin ________

La prima (koh-lah-tsee-oh-neh) **colazione è un poco differente** because it is fairly standardized **e Lei** will frequently take it at **il Suo albergo** as **è generalmente** included in **il prezzo della Sua camera. Sotto c'è** a sample of what **Lei può** expect to greet you **la** (maht-tee-nah) **mattina.** (in the morning)

Colazione 1 . . . . £800

caffelatte (coffee and steamed milk)
pane

(koh-lah-tsee-oh-neh) Colazione 2 . . . . £1,200

caffelatte
pane o (pah-nee-noh) **panino** (roll)
burro (butter) **e marmellata** (jam)

Colazione all'americana (in the American manner)

(these additions usually only available in large hotels catering to foreigners)

succo di arancia (orange juice)
succo di pompelmo (grapefruit)
prosciutto (ham)
salsiccia (sausage)

uova (egg) **affogate** (poached)
uova fritte (fried)
uova strapazzate (scrambled)
frittata (omelette)

Frasi pratiche

Quanto costa la prima colazione?

Vorrei due caffelatte, per piacere.

Vorrei dei (pah-nee-nee) **panini** (rolls) **e del tè, per favore.**

(vohr-rehb-beh) **Vorrebbe** (please) (fahr) **far** (have) (mohn-tah-reh) **montare** (brought up) **la prima colazione alla camera dieci, per favore.**

- ☐ **zero** *(zeh-roh)* . . . . zero ______
- ☐ **lo zodiaco** *(zoh-dee-ah-koh)* . . . . zodiac ______
  —Sono del segno acquario. . . . . I'm an Aquarius. ______
- ☐ **la zona** *(zoh-nah)* . . . . zone ______
- ☐ **lo zoo** *(zoh)* . . . . zoo ______

Step 19

Che è differente about **il telefono in Italia?** Well, **Lei** never notice such things until **Lei** want to use them. Be warned **adesso** that **telefoni in Italia** are less numerous than **in America.** Nevertheless, **il telefono** allows you to reserve **le camere d'albergo in** another **città** *(cheet-tah)* city, call **amici** *(ah-mee-chee)* friends, reserve **i biglietti di teatro, di concerto o di balletto** *(bahl-let-toh)* ballet, make emergency calls, check on the hours of a **museo** *(moo-seh-oh)* museum, rent **una macchina e** all those other **cose** which **facciamo** on a daily basis. It also gives you a certain amount of **libertà** *(lee-behr-tah)* **quando Lei può** make your own **telefonate** *(teh-leh-foh-nah-teh)* calls.

You may not always have **un telefono** in your **albergo in Italia.** This means that **Lei deve** *(deh-veh)* must **sapere dove trovare** to find **i telefoni:** in the **ufficio dei telefoni (S.I.P.)** *(seep)*, on the **strada,** in the **bar,** at the **stazione dei treni** and in the lobby of **il Suo albergo.** Often **Lei deve comprare** a token, called **un gettone** *(jet-toh-nee)*, to use when **Lei fa** make **una telefonata pubblica** *(poob-blee-kah)*.

Ecco un telefono pubblico *(poob-blee-koh)* **italiano.**

So far, so good. **Adesso,** let's read the instructions for using **il telefono.** This is one of those moments when you realize,

Non sono in America.

So let's learn how to operate **il telefono.**

If **Lei** use **il telefono in un bar,** be sure to ask, **"È necessario un gettone?"** *(neh-chehs-sah-ree-oh) (jet-toh-neh)* The **bar** employee will sell you **un gettone** to use if it is needed **e,** if not, then **Lei può** use regular **monete o una scheda telefonica.** *(skeh-dah) (teh-leh-foh-nee-kah)* (magnetic card)

TELEFONATA LOCALE:
Inserire (insert) **il gettone o le monete nella fessura** (opening)**. Alzare** (lift) **il ricevitore** (receiver) **e formare** (dial) **il numero.**
Aspettare (wait) **la risposta** (answer) **e premere** (press) **il pulsante** (push button) **che fa scendere** (makes fall) **il gettone.**
NEL CASO DI UNA TELEFONATA INTERURBANA (long-distance)**:**
Bisogna (it's necessary) **inserire almeno** (at least) **sei gettoni, £1·200 o la scheda.**
Quando la spia (light) **lampeggia** (flashes)**, bisogna inserire gettoni, monete o una nuova scheda.**
Alla (at the) **fine** (end) **della conversazione interurbana, i gettoni non usati** (unused) **verranno** (will be) **restituiti** (returned) **premendo** (pressing) **il pulsante appropriato di restituzione** (return)**.**

Inglese	Italiano
telephone	= **il telefono**
telephone booth	= **la cabina telefonica**
telephone book	= **l'elenco telefonico** *(leh-len-koh)*
telephone conversation	= **la conversazione telefonica**

Inglese	Italiano
to telephone	= **telefonare** *(teh-leh-foh-nah-reh)*
	= **fare una telefonata**
operator	= **l'operatore** *(loh-peh-rah-toh-reh)*
	= **la centralinista** *(chen-trah-lee-nee-stah)*
token	= **il gettone**

So **adesso Lei sa come fare una telefonata in Italia. Lei** will find that **la** *(mah-joh-rahn-tsah)* **maggioranza** (majority) **dei numeri in Italia sono sette** digits, such as **522-4500. Ci sono anche** area codes, or **i** *(noo-meh-ree)* **numeri** *(preh-fees-see)* **prefissi,** and these are listed in *(leh-len-koh)* **l'elenco** *(teh-leh-foh-nee-koh)* **telefonico** (telephone book).

When answering **il telefono, Lei** pick up **il** *(ree-cheh-vee-toh-reh)* **ricevitore** (receiver) **e** say:

"*(prohn-toh)* **Pronto! Sono** ______________ (il Suo nome)."

When saying good-bye, **Lei dice,** "**A** *(doh-mah-nee)* **domani**" (until tomorrow) **o** "**arrivederci.**" (good-bye) **Ecco** some sample **conversazioni al** (on the) **telefono.** Write them in the blanks **sotto.**

(voh-reh-ee) **Vorrei** (I would like) **telefonare all'Opera.** ______________

Vorrei telefonare a Chicago. Vorrei telefonare a Chicago.

Vorrei telefonare alla signora Sordini a Ostia. ______________

Vorrei telefonare al signor Sordini a San Remo. ______________

Vorrei telefonare a Alitalia all'aeroporto. ______________

Vorrei fare una telefonata "collect." ______________

Dov'è la cabina telefonica? ______________

Dov'è l'elenco telefonico. ______________

Il mio numero è 387-9106. ______________

(kwah-leh) **Qual'è** (what) **il Suo numero di telefono?** ______________

Qual'è il numero di telefono dell'albergo? ______________

Ecco *(oo-nahl-trah)* **un'altra** (another) **conversazione** *(pohs-see-bee-leh)* **possibile.** Listen to **le parole e come** they are used.

Thomas: **Pronto! Sono il signor Martini al telefono. Vorrei parlare alla signora Soleri.**

Segretaria: **Un momento, per favore. Mi scusi, ma la linea è occupata.**
but (ma)

Thomas: **Ripeta, per piacere. Parlo solamente un poco d'italiano. Parli più lentamente.**
(pee-oo) più = more; (len-tah-men-teh) lentamente = slowly

Segretaria: **Mi scusi, ma la linea è occupata.**

Thomas: **Beh. Grazie. Arrivederci, signorina.**
well (beh)

Ed ancora un'altra possibilità.
(pohs-see-bee-lee-tah)

Eva: **Vorrei delle informazioni per Assisi, per favore. Vorrei il numero di telefono del dottor Andrea Rossi, per piacere.**

Operatore: **Il numero è 816-4506.**

Eva: **Ripeta il numero, per favore.**

Operatore: **Il numero è 816-4506.**

Eva: **Molte grazie. Arrivederci.**

Operatore: **Prego. Arrivederci.**
you're welcome (prego)

Lei è adesso ready to use any **telefono in Italia.** Just take it **lentamente e** speak clearly.

Non dimenticati that **Lei può** ask . . .
(dee-men-tee-kee) non dimentichi = don't forget

Quanto costa una telefonata locale? *Quanto costa una telefonata locale?*
(loh-kah-leh) telefonata = call

Quanto costa una telefonata interurbana? ____________
(een-tair-oor-bah-nah) long-distance

Quanto costa una telefonata agli Stati Uniti? ____________
(ahl-yee) (stah-tee) (oo-nee-tee) agli = to the; Stati Uniti = United States

Quanto costa una telefonata interurbana a Firenze? ____________

Non dimentichi that **Lei ha bisogno di monete o di gettoni per il telefono.**
ha bisogno = need

Step 20

La metropolitana *(meh-troh-poh-lee-tah-nah)*, commonly called **"la metro** *(meh-troh)*," **è il nome per** the subway. **La metro a Roma è** a quick and cheap form of **trasporto** *(trah-spohr-toh)* [transportation], though not as extensive as the **sistema** *(see-steh-mah)* **di autobus.** The route **la metro** follows goes well outside the city limits into the **sobborghi** *(sohb-bohr-gee)* [suburbs] **di Roma. A Roma, e nelle** smaller **città** *(cheet-tah)* [cities], **c'è sempre** *(sem-preh)* [always] **l'autobus,** a slower but much more scenic means of **trasporto** *(trah-spohr-toh)*. **Lei** may also wish to go by **tassì.** In that case, find a taxi station, hail a **tassì** on the street or have one called **al Suo albergo. Quali** *(kwah-lee)* [what] **parole sono necessarie per viaggiare in metro, in autobus o in tassì?** Let's learn them by practicing them aloud **e poi** by writing them in the blanks **sotto.**

la metro *(meh-troh)* ____________________

il tassì *(tahs-see)* *il tassì*

l'autobus *(lah-oo-toh-boos)* ____________________

la fermata *(fehr-mah-tah)* = the stop ____________________

la linea *(lee-neh-ah)* = the line ____________________

il conduttore *(kohn-doot-toh-reh)* = the driver *il conduttore*

il controllore *(kohn-trohl-loh-reh)* = the ticket-collector ____________________

Let's also review **i verbi di trasporto** at this point.

salire *(sah-lee-reh)* = to board/to get into ____________________

scendere *(shehn-deh-reh)* = to get off/to go down *scendere*

cambiare *(kahm-bee-ah-reh)* **(autobus)** = to transfer (bus) ____________________

 viaggiare *(vee-ah-jah-reh)* = to travel ____________________

Maps displaying the various **linee e fermate** *(fehr-mah-teh)* **sono generalmente** posted outside every **entrata** *(en-trah-tah)* **della stazione** *(stah-tsee-oh-neh)* **della metro.** Almost every **pianta** *(pee-ahn-tah)* (map) **di Roma** also has a **metro** map included. To **comprare un biglietto, Lei** must put **monete** in a vending machine and the **biglietto** will come out. **Lei** take **il biglietto** and put it in the slot by the turnstile. When **Lei** cross through, **il biglietto** comes out. **Lei può** then **salire sul treno.** Check **il nome** of the **fermata** on the **linea** which you should take **e** catch **il treno** traveling in that **direzione.** *(dee-reh-tsee-oh-neh)* If **Lei deve cambiare treno** or transfer to an **autobus,** look for **le coincidenze** *(koh-een-chee-den-tseh)* (connections) clearly marked at each **fermata. Il sistema di autobus** works similarly. See **la pianta** *(pee-ahn-tah)* (map) **sotto.**

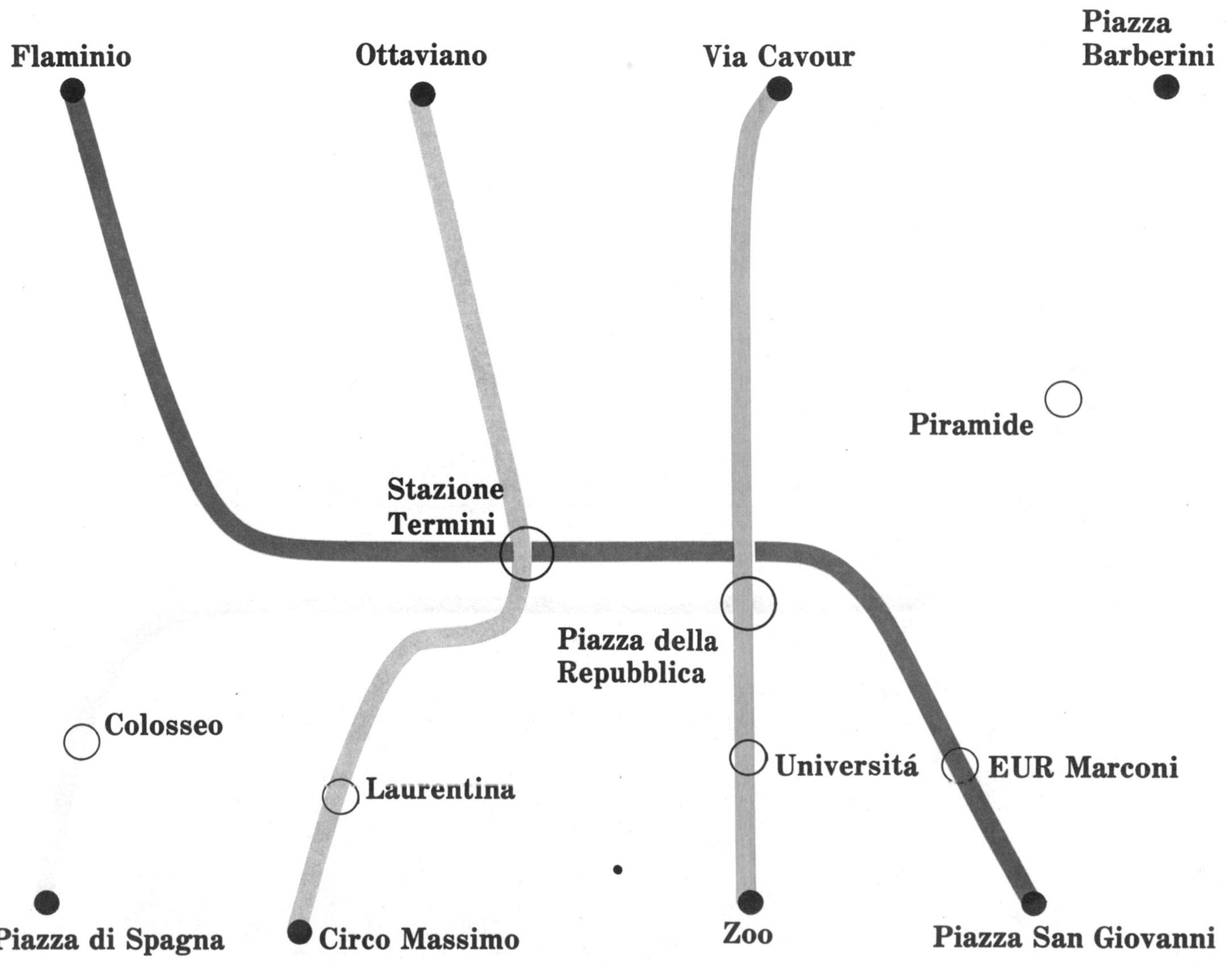

The same basic set of **parole e domande** will see you through traveling **in metro, in autobus, in macchina o** even **in treno.**

Naturally, la (pree-mah) **prima domanda è "dove."**

Dov'è la (fehr-mah-tah) **fermata della** (meh-troh) **metro?**

Dov'è la fermata dell'autobus?

Dov'è il (poh-steh-joh) **posteggio** (parking place) **dei tassì?**

Practice the following basic **domande** out loud **e poi** write them in the blanks **a destra.**

1. **Dov'è la fermata della metro?** ______________________

   Dov'è la fermata dell'autobus? *Dov'è la fermata dell'autobus?*

   Dov'è il (poh-steh-joh) **posteggio dei tassì?** ______________________

2. **Qual è la** (freh-kwen-tsah) **frequenza** (frequency) **dei treni per il Colosseo?** ______________________

   Qual è la frequenza degli autobus per il (vah-tee-kah-noh) **Vaticano?** ______________________

   Qual è la frequenza dei tassì per l'aeroporto? ______________________

3. (kwahn-doh) **Quando** (when) **parte il treno?** ______________________

   Quando parte l'autobus? ______________________

   Quando parte il tassì? ______________________

4. **Quando parte il treno per** (tee-voh-lee) **Tivoli?** ______________________

   Quando parte l'autobus per (pah-ree-oh-lee) **Parioli?** ______________________

   Quando parte il tassì per l'aeroporto? ______________________

5. **Quanto costa un biglietto della metro?** ______________________

   Quanto costa un biglietto dell'autobus? ______________________

   Quanto è la (tah-reef-fah) **tariffa?** (fare) *Quanto è la tariffa?*

   Quanto le (to you) (deh-voh) **devo?** (I owe) ______________________

Adesso that **Lei ha** gotten into the swing of things, practice the following patterns aloud, substituting **"autobus"** for **"metro" e** so on.

1. **Dove si compra un biglietto della metro? dell'autobus? del treno?**

2. **Quando parte il treno per il Foro Romano? per il centro** *(chen-troh)* **della città?** *(cheet-tah)* **per il Colosseo? per la Stazione Termini? per il Circo** *(cheer-koh)* **Massimo?** *(mahs-see-moh)*

3. **Dov'è la fermata della metro per andare al Piramide?** *(pee-rah-mee-deh)*

   Dov'è la fermata dell'autobus per andare al Foro Italico?

   Dov'è la fermata della metro per andare al centro della città?

   Dov'è la fermata dell'autobus per andare allo zoo? *(zoh)*

   Dov'è la fermata della metro per andare al Museo di Arte *(ahr-teh)* **Moderna?** *(moh-dair-nah)*

   Dov'è la fermata dell'autobus per andare a Piazza Venezia?

   Dov'è la fermata della metro per andare a Cinecittà? *(chee-neh-cheet-tah)*

   Dov'è la fermata dell'autobus per andare a Piazza Navona? *(nah-voh-nah)*

Legga *(lehg-gah)* [read] **la conversazione seguente, molto tipica, e la** [it] **scriva** in the blanks **a destra.**

Qual [which] **è la linea a Piazza Barberini?** *(bahr-beh-ree-nee)* ______________________

La linea gialla va a Piazza Barberini. ______________________

Con che frequenza? ______________________

Ogni *(ohn-yee)* [every] **cinque minuti.** Ogni cinque minuti.

Devo *(deh-voh)* **cambiare treno?** ______________________

Sí, alla Stazione Termini. Lei ha una coincidenza *(koh-een-chee-den-zah)* [connection] **alla Stazione Termini.**

Sí, alla Stazione Termini.

Quanti minuti ci *(chee)* [it] **vogliono** *(vohl-yoh-noh)* [takes] **per andare da** [from] **qui** *(kwee)* [here] **a Cinecittà?** *(chee-neh-cheet-tah)* ______________________

Ci [it] **vogliono** *(vohl-yoh-noh)* [takes] **20 minuti.** ______________________

Quanto costa il biglietto per Cinecittà? ______________________

Due cento lire. ______________________

Può Lei translate the following thoughts **in italiano? Le risposte sono sotto.**

1. Where is the subway stop? ______________________
2. What costs a ticket to Piazza Navona? ______________________
3. How often do the buses go to the airport? ______________________
4. Where does one buy a subway ticket? ______________________
5. Where is the bus stop? *Dov'è la fermata dell'autobus?*
6. I would like to get out. ______________________
7. Must I transfer? ______________________
8. Where must I transfer? ______________________

Ecco ancora tre verbi.

(lah-vah-reh) **lavare** = to wash	*(pehr-deh-reh)* **perdere** = to lose	*(chee)(voo-oh-leh)* **ci vuole** / *(chee)(vohl-yoh-noh)* **ci vogliono** = it takes
lavare	______________	______________

Lei know the basic "plug-in" formula, so translate the following thoughts **con questi nuovi verbi. Le risposte sono anche sotto.**

1. I wash the car. ______________________
2. You lose the book. ______________________
3. It takes 20 minutes to go to Parma. ______________________
4. It takes three hours by car. ______________________

RISPOSTE

1. **Dov'è la fermata della metro?**
2. **Quanto costa un biglietto per Piazza Navona?**
3. **Qual è la frequenza degli autobus per l'aeroporto?**
4. **Dove si compra un biglietto della metro?**
5. **Dov'è la fermata dell'autobus?**
6. **Vorrei scendere.**
7. **Devo cambiare?**
8. **Dove devo cambiare?**

---

1. **Lavo la macchina.**
2. **Perde il libro.**
3. **Ci vogliono venti minuti per andare a Parma.**
4. **Ci vogliono tre ore in macchina.**

Il Vendere (vehn-deh-reh) e il Comprare (kohm-prah-reh)

selling / buying

Shopping abroad **è** exciting. The simple everyday task of buying **un litro di latte o una mela** (meh-lah, apple) becomes a challenge that **Lei** should **adesso** be able to meet quickly **e** easily. Of course, **Lei** will purchase **dei ricordi** (ree-kohr-dee, souvenirs), **dei francobolli, e delle cartoline,** but **non dimentichi** (dee-men-tee-kee, forget) those many other **cose** ranging from shoelaces to **aspirina** (ah-spee-ree-nah, aspirin) that **Lei** might need unexpectedly. **Sa** (sah, know) **Lei la differenza fra una libreria** (lee-breh-ree-ah, bookstore) **e una macelleria** (mah-chehl-leh-ree-ah, butcher shop)**?** No. Let's learn about the different **negozi** (neh-goh-tsee, stores) **e botteghe** (boht-teh-geh, shops) **in Italia. Sotto c'è** (cheh) **una pianta** (pee-ahn-tah, map) **di una sezione** (seh-tsee-oh-neh, section) **di Roma.**

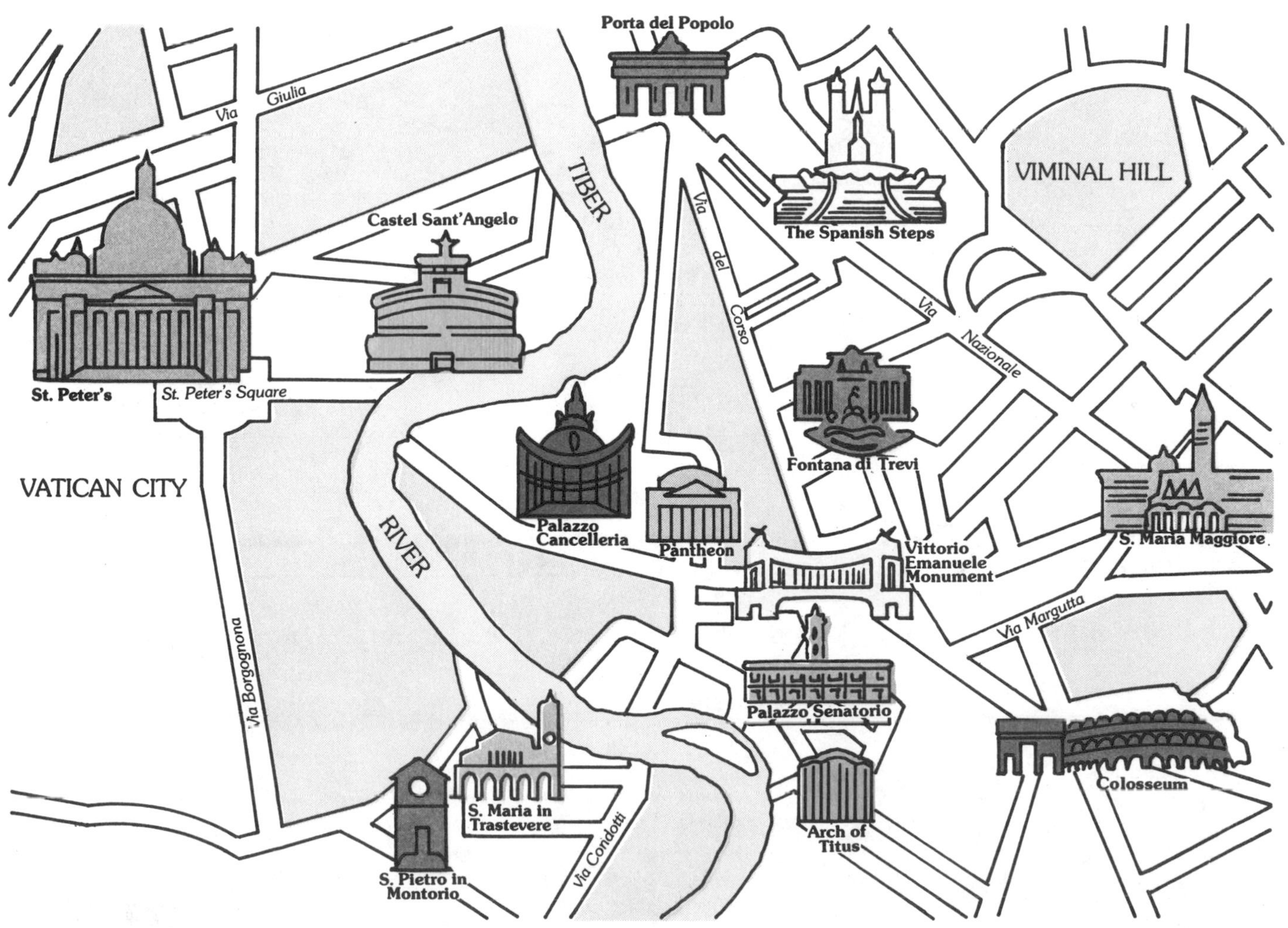

Alle pagine seguenti, ci sono all types of **negozi** (neh-goh-tsee) **in Italia.** Be sure to fill in the blanks **sotto le illustrazioni con il nome del** (of the) **negozio.**

il panificio, (pah-nee-fee-choh) bakery
dove si compra il pane (see) one buys

la macelleria, (mah-chel-leh-ree-ah) butcher shop
dove si compra la carne (see) one (kahr-neh)

la lavanderia, (lah-vahn-deh-ree-ah) laundry
dove si lavano i vestiti washes (veh-stee-tee)

la macelleria

il bar, (bahr)
dove si beve il caffè (beh-veh) drinks
o il vino o il whisky

la ferramenta, (fehr-rah-men-tah) hardware store
dove si compra la pila (pee-lah) battery

la farmacia, (fahr-mah-chee-ah) pharmacy
dove si compra l'aspirina (lah-spee-ree-nah)

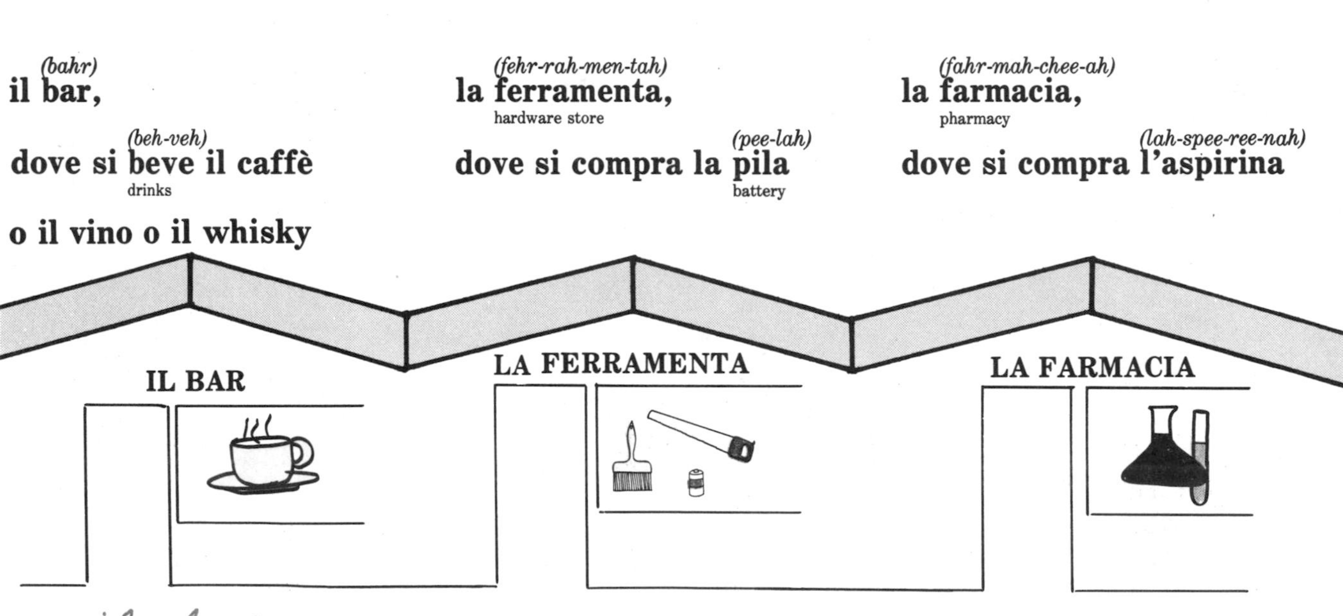

il bar

il fioraio, (fee-oh-rah-ee-oh) florist
dove si comprano i fiori

sali e tabacchi, dove si (sah-lee) salt (tah-bahk-kee) tobacco
compra il sale o
il tabacco

la confetteria, (kohn-fet-teh-ree-ah) candy store
dove si compra
il cioccolato (chok-koh-lah-toh)

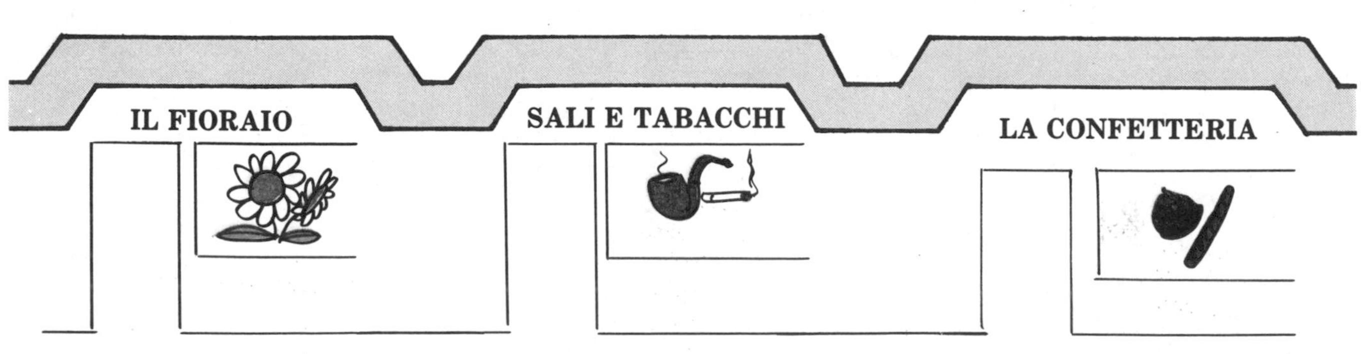

(laht-teh-ree-ah)
la latteria,
dairy

dove si compra il latte

(pah-stee-cheh-ree-ah)
la pasticceria,
pastry shop

(dohl-chee)
dove si comprano i dolci
sweets/pastries

(lehr-bee-ven-doh-loh)
l'erbivendolo,
greengrocer

(vehr-doo-reh)
dove si comprano le verdure
vegetables

(pahr-keh-joh)
il parcheggio,
parking lot

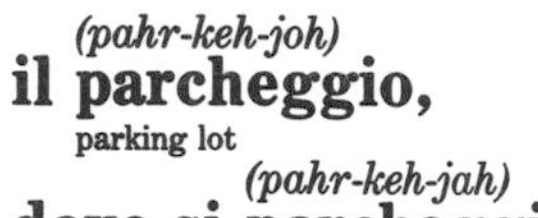

(pahr-keh-jah)
dove si parcheggia la
park

macchina

(pahr-rook-kee-eh-reh)
il parrucchiere,
hairdresser

(tahl-yah-noh)
dove si tagliano i
cut

(kah-pel-lee)
capelli
hair

(sahr-toh) *(sahr-tah)*
il sarto/la sarta,
tailor/seamstress

(fahn-noh) *(veh-stee-tee)*
dove si fanno i vestiti
make

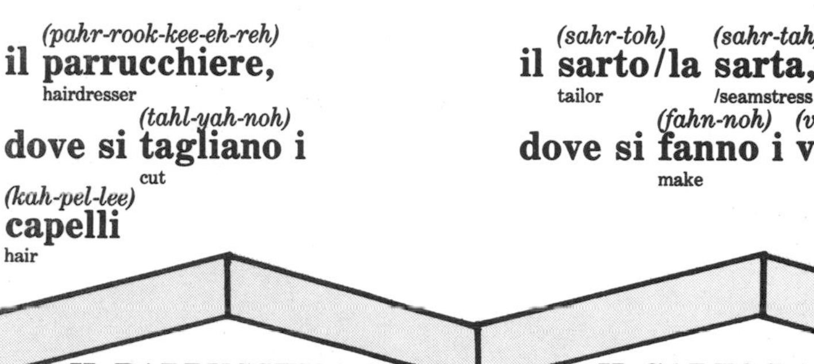

il sarto/la sarta

l'ufficio postale,
post office

dove si comprano i

francobolli

(kweh-stoo-rah)
la questura,
police station

(poh-lee-tsee-ah)
dove si trova la polizia
police

(bahn-kah)
la banca,
bank

dove si cambia
exchanges/cashes

il denaro

(soo-pehr-mehr-kah-toh)
il supermercato,
grocery store
dove si compra la carne o la frutta o il latte

(sah-loo-meh-ree-ah)
la salumeria,
delicatessen
(sah-loo-mee)
dove si comprano i salumi
sausages/salami

(froot-tee-ven-doh-loh)
il fruttivendolo,
fruit seller
(froot-tah)
dove si compra la frutta
fruit

(chee-neh-mah)
il cinema,
movie house
(veh-deh) (feelm)
dove si vede il film
sees

(johr-nah-lah-ee-oh)
il giornalaio,
newsstand
(johr-nah-lee)
dove si comprano i giornali
(ree-vee-steh)
e le riviste

(teen-toh-ree-ah)
la tintoria,
dry cleaner's
(lah-vah-joh)
dove si fa il lavaggio a
cleaning
(sehk-koh)
secco
dry

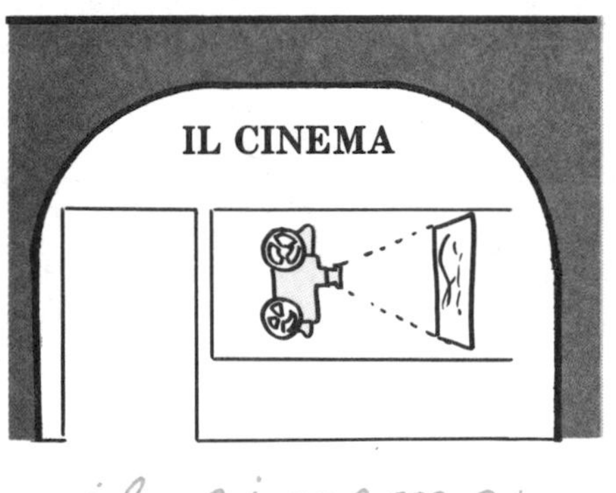

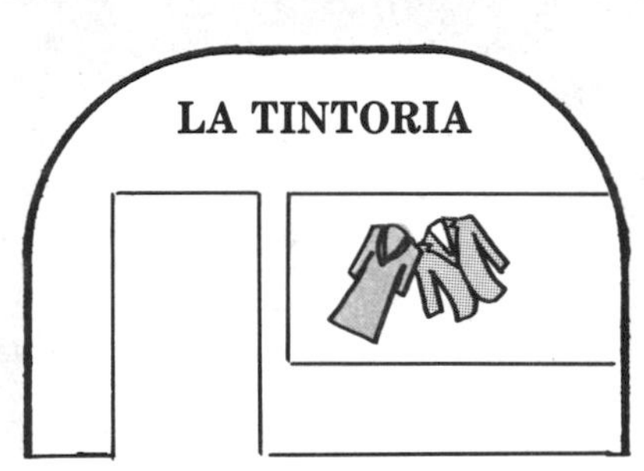

il cinema

(kahr-toh-leh-ree-ah)
la cartoleria,
stationery store
dove si compra la carta, o la penna o la matita

(lee-breh-ree-ah)
la libreria,
bookstore
dove si comprano e si vendono i libri

(mah-gah-tsee-noh)
il grande magazzino,
department store
(toot-toh)
dove si compra tutto
everything
(see Step 22)

LA CARTOLERIA

LA LIBRERIA

IL GRANDE MAGAZZINO

(mehr-kah-toh)
il mercato, dove si comprano
market
la verdura e la frutta

(lee-pehr-mehr-kah-toh)
l'ipermercato
supermarket
dove si compra tutto
everything

l'ipermercato

(stah-tsee-on-neh)
la stazione di benzina,
gas station
dove si compra la benzina

(lah-jehn-tsee-ah) (vee-ah-jee)
l'agenzia di viaggi,
travel agency
dove si compra un biglietto dell'aeroplano

(loh-roh-loh-jeh-ree-ah)
l'orologeria,
clock and watchmaker's shop
dove si comprano gli orologi

(peh-skeh-ree-ah)
la pescheria,
fish market
(peh-sheh)
dove si compra il pesce
fish

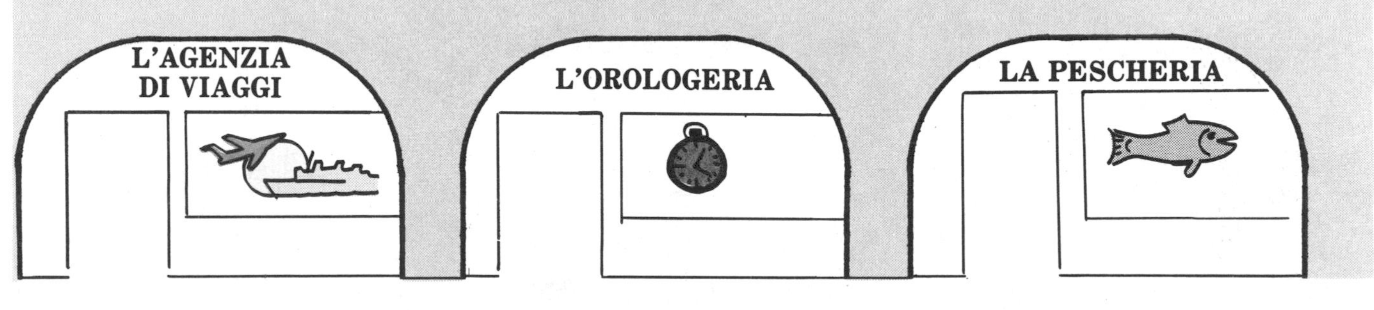

(ah-pehr-tee) (neh-goh-tsee)
Quando sono aperti i negozi italiani? I negozi italiani sono generalmente aperti da lunedì a sabato, dalle 9,00 alle 18,30. Molti negozi will close over the lunch hour **(12,30 — 15,00).** Many shops **sono anche** closed **il lunedì.** Local, open-air **mercati sono** truly **un'esperienza,** so be sure to check **le ore** of the one closest to **il Suo albergo.**

(are / open / stores; *(oo-neh-speh-ree-en-zah)* experience; *(leh) (oh-reh)* hours)

C'è anything else which makes **i negozi italiani differenti** from **i negozi americani? Sí.**
is there
Look at **le illustrazioni alla pagina seguente.**

In Italia, the ground floor **si chiama "il** *(pee-ahn-tehr-reh-noh)* **pianterreno."** The first floor **è** the next floor up **e** so on. Now that **Lei** know **i nomi dei negozi italiani,** let's practice shopping.

I. First step — Dove?

Dov'è la latteria?   **Dov'è la banca?**   **Dov'è il cinema?**

Go through **i negozi** introduced in this Step **e** ask **"Dove" con** *(ohn-yee)* **ogni** (each) **negozio.** Another way of asking **dove** is to ask

(cheh) **C'è** (is there) **una latteria** *(kwee)* **qui** (here) *(vee-chee-noh)* **vicino?** (near)   **C'è una banca qui vicino?**

Go through **i negozi** again using *(kwehs-tah)* **questa** (this) **nuova domanda.**

II. Next step — tell them what Lei are looking for, need o vorrebbe!

1) *(oh)* **Ho** *(bee-sohn-yoh)* **bisogno di . . .** Ho bisogno di ____________________

2) **Ha Lei . . . ?** ____________________

3) **Vorrei . . .** ____________________

Ho bisogno di una matita.

Ha Lei una matita?

Vorrei una matita.

Ho bisogno di un chilo *(kee-loh)* **di mele** *(meh-leh)***.**

Ha Lei un chilo di mele?

Vorrei un chilo di mele.

Go through the glossary at the end of **questo libro e** select **venti parole.** Drill the above patterns **con questi venti parole.** Don't cheat. Drill them **oggi. Adesso,** take **ancora** (more) **venti parole dal Suo** glossary **e** do the same.

III. Next step — find out **quanto costa.**

1) **Quanto è?** ______________________________

2) **Quanto costa?** ______________________________

Quanto costa la matita?

Quanto costa una cartolina?

Quanto costa il francobollo?

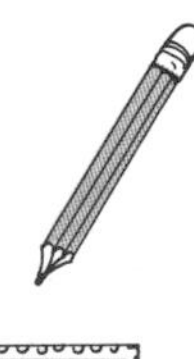

Quanto costa un chilo di mele?

Quanto costa un chilo di arance *(ah-rahn-cheh)***?**

Quanto costa un chilo di carne?

Using these same **parole** that **Lei** selected **sopra,** drill **anche queste domande.**

IV. If **Lei non sa dove trovare** something, **Lei domanda** (ask)

Dove si compra l'aspirina *(lah-spee-ree-nah)***?**

Dove si comprano gli occhiali *(ohk-kee-ah-lee)* **da sole** *(soh-leh)***?** (sunglasses)

Once **Lei trova** what **Lei** would like, **Lei dice,** **Vorrei questo, per favore.**

O, if Lei would not like it, **Non vorrei questo, grazie.**

Adesso Lei è all set to shop for anything!

Step 22

Il Grande Magazzino

(grahn-deh) (mah-gah-tsee-noh) — department store

At this point, **Lei** should just about be ready for **il Suo viaggio in Italia. Lei** have gone shopping for those last-minute odds 'n ends. Most likely, the store directory at your local **grande magazzino** (mah-gah-tsee-noh) did not look like the one **sotto. Lei** already know **molte parole e Lei può** guess at **molte altre** (ahl-treh) (others). **Lei sa che "bambino"** (bahm-bee-noh) **significa** (seen-yee-fee-kah) (means) "child," so if **Lei ha bisogno di** something **per un bambino, Lei** would probably look on the **secondo o terzo piano, vero?**

Piano			
6. PIANO	alimentari tavola calda salumeria	pollame frutta verdura prodotti surgelati	vino cacciagione carne
5. PIANO	letti lenzuoli specchi	mobili lampade tappeti	quadri elettrodomestici
4. PIANO	cristalleria vasellame da cucina	servizi da tavola mobili da cucina	chiavi ceramica porcellana
3. PIANO	libri televisori mobili da bambini giocattoli	radio strumenti musicali cartoleria dischi	ristorante giornali riviste
2. PIANO	tutto per il bambino vestiti da donna cappelli da donna	vestiti da uomo scarpe da bambino foto	gabinetti antiquario
1. PIANO	accessori da macchina fazzoletti biancheria	costumi da bagno scarpe da donna scarpe da uomo	articoli sportivi articoli da campeggio ferramenta
P	ombrelli biglietti di auguri cappelli da uomo gioielleria	guanti articoli di pelle e cuoio calze	cinture orologi profumeria pasticceria

Let's start a checklist **per il Suo viaggio.** Besides **vestiti** (veh-stee-tee) (clothing), **di che** (keh) **ha bisogno** (bee-sohn-yoh) **Lei?**

 Che è necessario in Europa?

il passaporto *(pahs-sah-pohr-toh)*

il biglietto *(beel-yet-toh)*

la valigia *(vah-lee-jah)* — la valigia ✓

la borsa *(bohr-sah)*

il portafoglio *(pohr-tah-fohl-yoh)*

il denaro *(deh-nah-roh)*

la macchina fotografica *(mahk-kee-nah foh-toh-grah-fee-kah)*

la pellicola *(pel-lee-koh-lah)*

Prenda *(prehn-dah)* (take) **gli otto prossimi** labels **e** label **queste cose oggi.** Better yet, assemble them **in un angolo della Sua casa.**

Viaggia Lei in Italia in estate o in inverno? Non (don't) **dimentichi...** *(dee-men-tee-kee)* (forget)

i costumi da bagno *(koh-stoo-mee bahn-yoh)*

i sandali *(sahn-dah-lee)*

Non dimentichi neanche *(neh-ahn-keh)* (either) the basic toiletries!

il sapone *(sah-poh-neh)* — il sapone ✓

lo spazzolino da denti *(spah-tsoh-lee-noh den-tee)*

il dentifricio *(den-tee-free-choh)*

il rasoio *(rah-soh-ee-oh)*

il deodorante *(deh-oh-doh-rahn-teh)*

il pettine *(pet-tee-neh)*

For the rest of the **cose,** let's start **con** the outside layers **e** work our way in.

(soh-prah-bee-toh)
il soprabito ________________

(leem-pehr-meh-ah-bee-leh)
l'impermeabile ________________

(lohm-brel-loh)
l'ombrello ________________

(gwahn-tee)
i guanti ________________

(kahp-pel-loh)
il cappello ________________

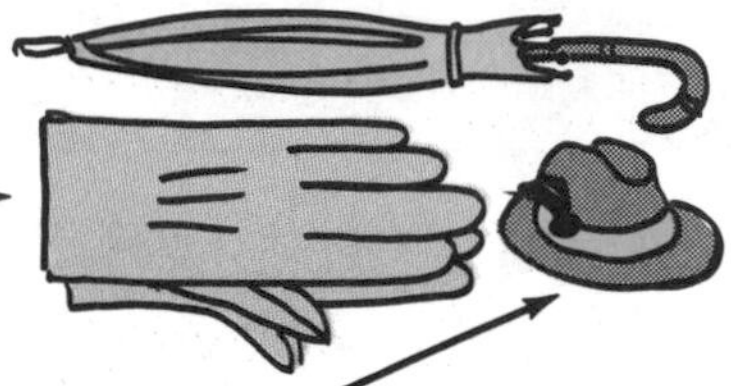

(stee-vah-leh)
lo stivale ________________ lo stivale

(skahr-pah)
la scarpa ________________

(kahl-tsee-noh)
il calzino ________________

(kahl-tseh)
le calze ________________

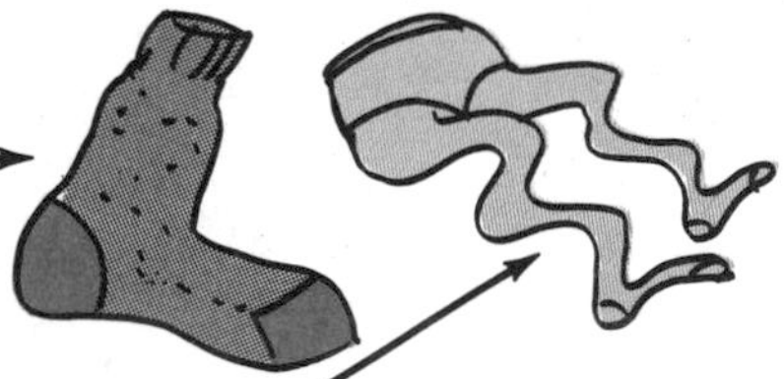

(prehn-dah) **Prenda** (take) **i** next group of labels **e** label **queste cose** today. Check **e** make sure that **sono** (poo-lee-tee) **puliti** (clean) **e** ready **per il Suo viaggio.** Check them off on **questa lista** as **Lei** organize them. From now on, **Lei ha il** (den-tee-free-choh) **"dentifricio" e non il** "toothpaste."

(pee-jah-mah)
il pigiama ________________ il pigiama

(kah-mee-chet-tah) (noht-teh)
la camicetta da notte ________________

(lahk-kahp-pah-toh-ee-oh)
L'accappatoio (bathrobe) ________________

(pahn-toh-foh-leh)
le pantofole ________________

(lahk-kahp-pah-toh-ee-oh) **L'accappatoio** (bathrobe) **e le pantofole** (slippers) (pohs-soh-noh) **possono** (can) **anche** double **per Lei alla** (spee-ah-jah) **spiaggia.** (beach)

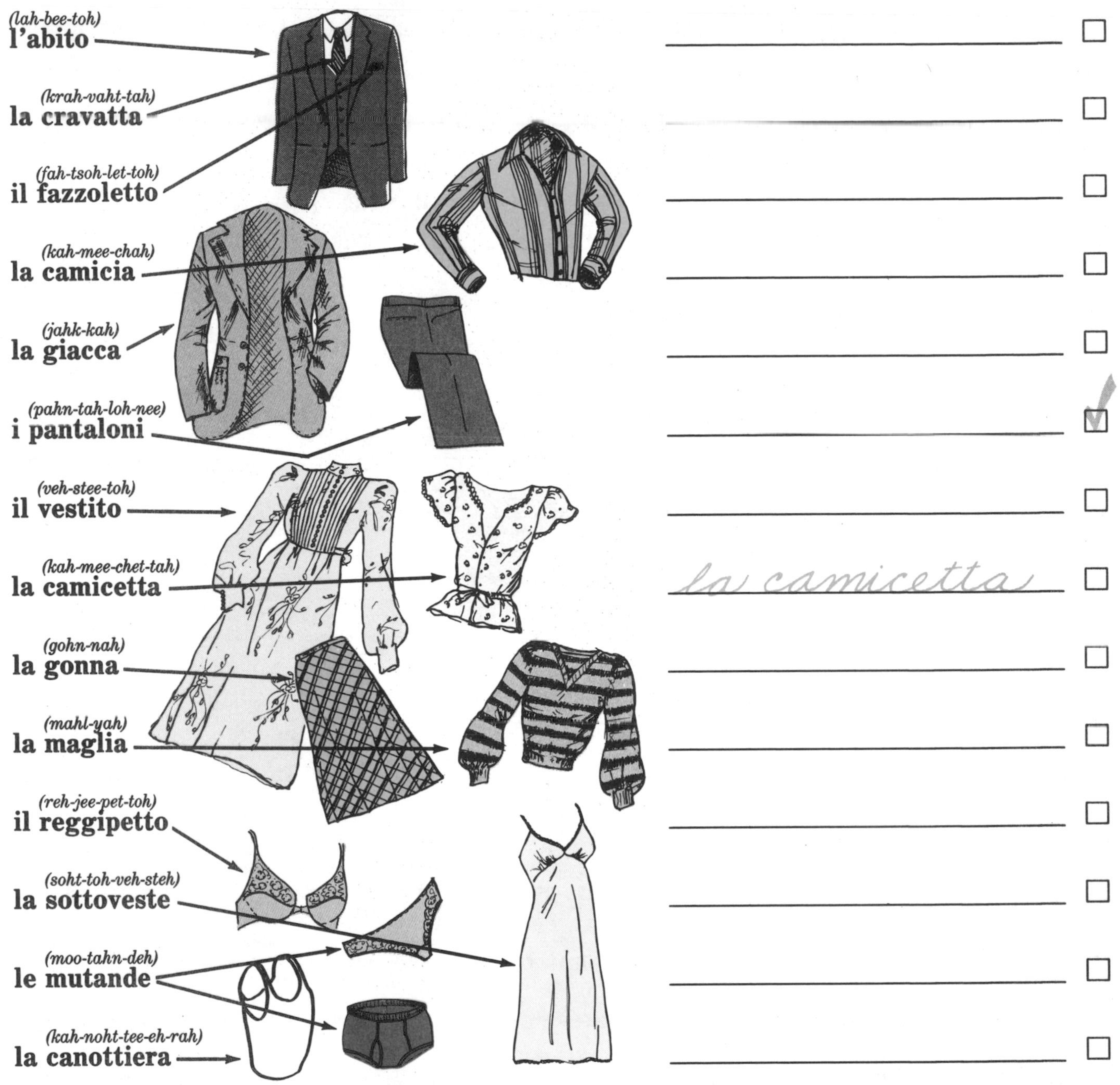

Having assembled **queste cose, Lei è pronto per il Suo viaggio.** However, being human means occasionally forgetting something. Look again at **il grande magazzino** directory.

(queste = these; pronto *(prohn-toh)* = ready)

A quale piano Lei trova . . . (piano = floor)

vestiti da uomo? *(oo-oh-moh)* (uomo = man) — **Al** ______________ **piano.**

un cappello per una donna? — **Al** ______________ **piano.**

libri? — **Al** ______________ **piano.**

biancheria? *(bee-ahn-keh-ree-ah)* (biancheria = lingerie) — **Al** ______________ **piano.**

(kree-stahl-lair-ee-ah)
cristalleria? **Al** ______________________ **piano.**

(proh-foo-mair-ee-ah)
profumeria? **Al** ______________________.

vestiti da donna? **Al** ______________________ **piano.**

Adesso, just remember your basic **domande. Ripeta la conversazione tipica sotto** out loud **e poi** by filling in the blanks.

Dove si trovano i pantaloni da donna? ______________________

(reh-pahr-toh)
Nel reparto dei vestiti da donna. ______________________
department

Dov'è il reparto dei vestiti da donna? ______________________

Al secondo piano. al secondo piano.

Dove si trovano il sapone ed il dentifricio? ______________________

Al pianterreno. ______________________

(doh-mahn-dah-reh)
Anche, non dimentichi di domandare . . .
to ask

(lah-shen-soh-reh)
Dov'è l'ascensore? ______________________
elevator

(skah-leh)
Dove sono le scale? ______________________
stairs

(moh-bee-leh)
Dov'è la scala mobile? ______________________
escalator

(oo-oh-moh)
Whether **Lei ha bisogno di pantaloni da donna o di una camicia da uomo, le parole necessarie sono** the same. Practice your **nuove parole con i vestiti seguenti. Dov'è la gonna? Dov'è...**

Che *(tahl-yah)* **taglia?** (size)

Che *(mee-soo-rah)* **misura?** (size for shoes and gloves)

Questo *(mee)* **mi** (me) *(vah)* **va.** (fits)

Questo mi va.

Questo non mi va.

(prehn-doh) **Prendo** (I take) **questo.** (this)

Quanto è?

È (that's) *(toot-toh)* **tutto,** (all) **grazie.**

Clothing sizes: *(dohn-neh)* **DONNE** (women)

scarpe									
American	5	5½	6	6½	7	7½	8	8½	9
Continental	35	35	36	37	38	38	38	39	40

vestiti						
American	8	10	12	14	16	18
Continental	36	38	40	42	44	46

camicette, maglie							
American	32	34	36	38	40	42	44
Continental	40	42	44	46	48	50	52

Clothing sizes: *(oo-oh-mee-nee)* **UOMINI** (men)

scarpe										
American	7	7½	8	8½	9	9½	10	10½	11	11½
Continental	39	40	41	42	43	43	44	44	45	45

vestiti								
American	34	36	38	40	42	44	46	48
Continental	44	46	48	50	52	54	56	58

camicie								
American	14	14½	15	15½	16	16½	17	17½
Continental	36	37	38	39	40	41	42	43

Adesso, Lei è pronto per il Suo viaggio. Lei sa tutto that you need. The next Step will give you a quick review of international road signs **e** then **Lei** are off to **l'aeroporto.**

Buon viaggio! Buon divertimento!

Step 23

= **Dangerous Intersection**

Ecco some of the most important **segnali** *(sen-yah-lee)* [signs] **stradali** *(strah-dah-lee)* [road] **internazionali** *(een-tehr-nah-tsee-oh-nah-lee)* [international]. Remember that **in Italia** a basic rule of the road is **priorità** *(pree-oh-ree-tah)* [yield] **a** [to] **destra** [the right]. **Guidi** *(gwee-dee)* [drive] **attentamente!** *(aht-ten-tah-men-teh)* [carefully] **Buon viaggio!**

1 EUROPA

Danger

Dangerous curve

Dangerous intersection

Closed to all vehicles

Prohibited for motor vehicles

Prohibited for motor vehicles on Sundays and holidays

No entry

Stop

Main road ahead, yield the right of way

You have the right of way

Additional sign indicating the right of way

One-way street

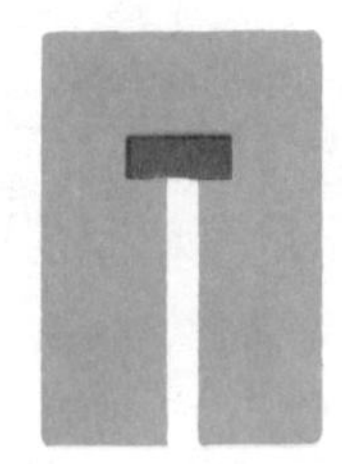

Dead-end street

Detour

Traffic circle

No left turn

No U-turn

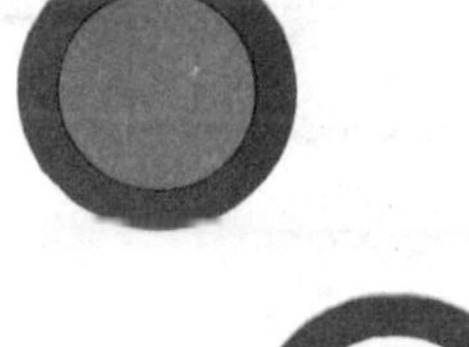

No parking

No parking or waiting

No passing

Speed limit

End of speed limit

Beginning of **autostrada**

Railroad crossing
240 meters

Railroad crossing
160 meters

Railroad crossing
80 meters

Customs

Federal Highway
Number

City limit

End of city limit

Parking permitted

Road ends, water
ahead

GLOSSARY

A

a . . . . . at, to
a domani . . . . . until tomorrow
abbiamo/avere . . . . . we have/to have
abitare . . . . . to live, to reside
abito, l' . . . . . suit
accanto a . . . . . next to
accappatoio, l' . . . . . bathrobe
accelerato, l' . . . . . slow train
acqua, l' . . . . . water
adesso . . . . . now
aereo, l'; aereoplano, l' . . . . . airplane
aereoporto, l' . . . . . airport
agenzia di noleggio, l' . car rental agency
agenzia di viaggi, l' . . . . . travel agency
agli . . . . . to the
agnello, l' . . . . . lamb
agosto . . . . . August
al forno . . . . . baked
albergatore, l' . . . . . hotelkeeper
albergo, l' . . . . . hotel
alcool, l' . . . . . alcohol
alcune, alcuni . . . . . some
alfabeto, l' . . . . . alphabet
alla griglia . . . . . grilled
al, alla, alle, allo . . . . . to the, at the
almeno . . . . . at least
alte, alto . . . . . high
altre, altro . . . . . others
alzare . . . . . to lift
America, l' . . . . . America
americano, l' . . . . . American
amica, l'; amico, l' (gli amici) . . . . friend
anche, anch' . . . . . also
ancora . . . . . more, still
andare . . . . . to go
andata e ritorno . . . . . round-trip
angolo, l' . . . . . corner
anno, l' . . . . . year
antipasti, gli . . . . . appetizers
aperto . . . . . open
appetito, l' . . . . . appetite
appuntamenti, gli . . . . . appointments
apra . . . . . open
aprile . . . . . April
arancia, l' (le arance) . . . . . orange
aranciata, l' . . . . . orangeade
armadietto di cucina, l' . . . . . cupboard
armadio, l' . . . . . wardrobe
arriva/arrivare . . arrive, arrives/to arrive
arriverderci . . . . . good-bye
arrivo, l' . . . . . arrival
arrosto . . . . . roasted
ascensore, l' . . . . . elevator
asciugamani, gli . . . . . towels
  asciugamano da bagno, l' . . bath towel
  asciugamano grande, l' . . . . large towel
  asciugamano piccolo, l' . . . . hand towel
aspettare . . . . . to wait for
aspirina, l' . . . . . aspirin
attentamente . . . . . carefully
attenzione, l' . . . . . attention
atterrare . . . . . to land
attore, l' . . . . . actor
attraverso . . . . . across
auto, l' . . . . . car
autobus, l' . . . . . bus
autostrada, l' . . . . . highway
autunno, l' . . . . . autumn
avere . . . . . to have
avere bisogno di . . . . . to need
azzurro . . . . . blue

B

bagagli, i . . . . . bags, suitcases
bagnarsi . . . . . to bathe
balleto, il . . . . . ballet
bambino, il (i bambini) . . . . . child
banana, la . . . . . banana
banca, la . . . . . bank
bar, il . . . . . bar, pub
barca, la . . . . . boat
basato . . . . . based
basso, bassa . . . . . low
beh . . . . . oh, well
bel, bella, bello . . . . . nice, beautiful
bene . . . . . good
benedizione, la . . . . . benediction
benzina, la . . . . . gas
bere . . . . . to drink
bevande, le . . . . . beverages
biancheria, la . . . . . lingerie
bianco . . . . . white
bicchiere, il (i bicchieri) . . . . . glass
bicicletta, la . . . . . bicycle
biglietto, il (i biglietti) . . . . . bank note, bill, ticket
  biglietti dell'autobus, i . . . . bus tickets
  biglietti teatrali, i . . . . . theater tickets
binario, il . . . . . train track
birra, la (le birre) . . . . . beer
bisogno, il . . . . . need
bistecca, la . . . . . steak
bolle . . . . . boils
borsa, la . . . . . handbag, purse
botteghe, le . . . . . stores, shops
bottiglia, la . . . . . bottle
breve . . . . . brief, short
buca delle lettere, la . . . . . mailbox
buon, buona, buono . . . . . good
  buona fortuna . . . . . good luck
  buon giorno . . . . . good morning, good afternoon
  buona notte . . . . . good night
  buona sera . . . . . good evening
  buon viaggio . . . . . have a good trip!
burro, il . . . . . butter

C

cabina telefonica, la . . . telephone booth
cacciagione, la . . . . . wild game
caffè, il . . . . . coffee
  caffelatte, il . . coffee and steamed milk
caldo . . . . . warm, hot
calendario, il . . . . . calendar
calze, le . . . . . nylon stockings
calzino, il (i calzini) . . . . . sock
cambiare (treno) . . . . . to transfer (train)
camera, la . . . . . room
camera da letto, la . . . . . bedroom
cameriera, la . . . . . waitress
cameriere, il . . . . . waiter
camicetta, la . . . . . blouse
camicetta da notte, la . . . . . nightshirt
camicia, la . . . . . shirt
campanello, il . . . . . doorbell
cane, il . . . . . dog
canottiera, la . . . . . undershirt
cantina, la . . . . . cellar
capelli, i . . . . . hair
capire . . . . . to understand
cappello, il . . . . . hat
cappotto, il . . . . . overcoat
cara, caro . . . . . expensive
caramelle, le . . . . . caramels, candies
carne, la . . . . . meat
carta, la . . . . . paper, map
cartoleria, la . . . . . stationery store
cartolina, la . . . . . postcard
casa, la . . . . . house
cassa, la . . . . . cashier's desk
castello, il . . . . . castle
categoria, la . . . . . category
cattedrale, la . . . . . cathedral
cattivo . . . . . bad
cattolica . . . . . Catholic
c'è . . . . . there is
cena, la . . . . . dinner
cento . . . . . one hundred
centralinista, la . . . . . telephone operator
centro, il . . . . . center, downtown
certo . . . . . certainly
cestino, il . . . . . wastebasket
che . . . . . what
chi . . . . . who
chiama/chiamarsi . . call, calls/to be called
chiesa, la . . . . . church
chili, i . . . . . kilos
chiuso . . . . . closed
ci sono . . . . . there are
ci vogliono, ci vuole . . . . . it takes
ciao . . . . . hi!/bye!
cinema, il . . . . . cinema, movie house
cinquanta . . . . . fifty
cinque . . . . . five
cioccolato, il . . . . . chocolate
cioccolata, la . . . . . hot chocolate
città, la . . . . . city
coincidenze, le . . . . . train connections
colazione, la . . . . . breakfast, lunch
colore, il (i colori) . . . . . color
coltello, il . . . . . knife
come . . . . . how
comincia . . . . . begin, begins
compra, comprano/comprare . . . . . buy, buys/to buy
comunicazione, la . . . . . communication
con . . . . . with
concerto, il . . . . . concert
conduttore, il . . . . . driver
confetteria, la . . . . . candy store
continui . . . . . continue
conto, il . . . . . bill
contorni, i . . . . . vegetables
contravvenzione, la . . . . . traffic ticket
controllore, il . . . . . ticket-collector
conversazione, la . . . . . conversation
coperta, la . . . . . blanket
corretto . . . . . correct
corridoio, il . . . . . hallway
corta, corto . . . . . short
cose, le . . . . . things
costa/costare . . . . . cost, costs/to cost
costume, il . . . . . custom
cotto . . . . . cooked
cravatta, la . . . . . tie
cuccetta, la . . . . . berths
cucchiaio, il . . . . . spoon
cucina, la . . . . . kitchen
costume da bagno, il . . . . . bathing suit
cristallo, il . . . . . crystal
cucina, la . . . . . kitchen, stove
cugina, la; cugino, il . . . . . cousin
cuoco, il . . . . . cook
cuscino, il . . . . . pillow

D

da . . . . . of, from
dal, dalla . . . . . from the
davanti a . . . . . in front of
decorato . . . . . decorated
degli, dei, del, delle . . . . . some, of the
denaro, il . . . . . money
delizioso . . . . . delicious
dentrifricio, il . . . . . toothpaste

deodorante, il .... deodorant
desidera .... desire, desires
desserti, i .... desserts
destra .... right
a destra .... to the right
deve/dovere ....
..... should, owe, owes/to have to, to owe
deviazione, la .... detour
di .... of, in
di nuovo .... again
dicembre .... December
diciannove .... nineteen
diciassette .... seventeen
dieci .... ten
diciotto .... eighteen
dietro .... behind
differente, differenti .... different
difficile .... difficult
dimentichi .... forget
dire .... to say
direttissimo, il; diretto, il ..... fast train
diretto .... direct
direzione, la (le direzioni) .... direction
diritto .... straight ahead
distanza, la .... distance
divertimento, il .... fun
dizionario, il .... dictionary
dodici .... twelve
doccia, la .... shower
dogana, la .... customs
dolce, il .... pastry, sweet
dollaro, il .... dollar
domanda, la (le domande) ..... question
domani .... tomorrow
domenica .... Sunday
donna, la (le donne) .... woman
dopo .... after
dormire .... to sleep
dottore, il .... doctor
dove .... where
dov'è .... where is
dove sono .... where are
dovere .... to have to/to owe
dubbio, il .... doubt
due .... two
durante .... during

E

è .... is
e .... and
e mezzo .... half past
e un quarto .... a quarter past
ebraica, ebreo .... Jewish
eccellente .... excellent
ecco .... here is, there is
economica .... inexpensive
ed .... and
elefante, l' .... elephant
elenco telefonico, l' ..... telephone book
entra/entrare ..... enter, enters/to enter
entrata, l' .... entrance
entrata principale, l' ... main entrance
entrata laterale, l' ...... side entrance
erba, l' .... grass
erbivendolo, l' .... green grocer
esempio, l' (gli esempi) .... example
espressioni, le .... expressions
espresso, l' .... very fast train
est, l' .... east
dell'est .... eastern
estate, l' .... summer
Europa, l' .... Europe

F

FS, le ... . Italian national railroad
fa/fare ....
.... do, does; make, makes/to do, to make
facchino, il .... porter
facile .... easy
fame, la .... hunger
famiglia, la .... family
farcito .... stuffed
fare .... to do, to make
farmacia, la ...... pharmacy, drugstore
favore, il .... favor
per favore .... please
fazzoletto, il .... handkerchief
Febbraio .... February
fede, la .... faith
fermata, la (le fermate) .... stop
ferramenta, la .... hardware store
ferrovia, la (le ferrovie) .... railroad
fessura, la .... opening
figli, i .... children
figlia, la .... daughter
figlio, il .... son
film, il .... film
finalmente .... finally
fine, la .... end
finestra, la .... window
fioraio, il .... florist
fiore, il (i fiori) .... flower
fisso .... fixed
foglio, il (i fogli) .... piece
fontana, la .... fountain
forchetta, la .... fork
foresta, la .... forest
forma, la .... form
formaggio, il .... cheese
formare ....dial (the telephone)
forte .... loudly
fortuna, la .... luck
fra .... between
Francia, la .... France
francobollo, il .... stamp
frase, la (le frasi) .... phrase
fratello .... brother
freddo .... cold
frequenza, la .... frequency
fresco .... cool, fresh
frigorifero, il .... refrigerator
fritto .... fried
frutta, la .... fruit
fruttivendolo, il .... fruit seller
fumare .... to smoke

G

gabinetto, il (i gabinetti) ...... lavatory
garage, il .... garage
gatto, il .... cat
gela .... freezes
generalmente .... generally
genitori, i .... parents
gennaio .... January
gentilezza, la .... politeness
gettone, il .... token (for telephone calls)
giacca, la .... jacket
giallo .... yellow
giardino, il .... garden
giornalaio, il ....
.... newspaper and magazine vendor
giornale, il .... newspaper
giorno, il, (i giorni) .... day
giovane .... young
giovedì .... Thursday
giri .... turn
giugno .... June
gli .... the
gondola, la .... Venetian boat
gonna, la .... skirt
gradi .... degrees
grande .... grand, big, large
grande magazzino, il ...department store
grazie .... thank you
grigio .... gray
grosso .... thick
guanto, il (i guanti) .... glove
guanto da bagno, il .... washglove
guardi .... look at
guida, la .... guide
guidare .... to drive

H

ho/avere .... I have/to have

I

idea, l' .... idea
identiche, identico .... identical
ieri .... yesterday
illustrazioni, le .... pictures
immaginazione, l' .... imagination
impari/imparare .... learn/to learn
impermeabile, l' .... raincoat
ipermercato, l' .... supermarket
importante .... important
in .... in, into
indirizzo, l' .... address
individuale .... individual, single
influenza, l' .... influence, influenza
informazione, l' .... information
Inghilterra, l' .... England
inglese .... English
ingresso, l' .... entrance
insalata, l' .... salad
inserire .... to insert
inverno, l' .... winter
io I
io sono .... I am
Italia .... Italy
Italiani, gli .... Italians
italiano .... Italian

L

l' ....the
lampada, la .... lamp
latte, il .... milk
latteria, la .... dairy
lavanderia, la .... laundry
lavandino, il .... sink
lavare .... to wash
legume, il .... vegetable
leggere .... to read
lei .... she
Lei .... you
lentamente .... slowly
lento .... slow
lettera, la .... letter
letto, il .... bed
lezione, la .... lesson, lecture
libro, il .... book
lì .... there
libreria, la .... bookstore
linea, la (le linee) .... line
lira .... Italian unit of currency
lista, la .... list, menu
litro, il (i litri) .... liter
lo .... it, the
loro .... they
luce, la .... light
luglio .... July
lui .... he, him
lunedì .... Monday
lunga, lungo .... long
loro .... they

M

ma .... but
macchina, la .... car

macchina da noleggiare, la ... rental car
macchina fotografica, la .... camera
macelleria, la .... butcher shop
madre, la .... mother
maggio .... May
maggioranza, la .... majority
maglia, la .... sweater
maiale, il .... pork
malato .... sick
male .... bad
mancia, la .... tip
mandare .... to send
mangiare .... to eat
mano, la .... hand
manzo, il .... beef
marciapiede, il .... railway platform
marrone .... brown
marzo .... March
martedì .... Tuesday
matita, la .... pencil
mattina, la .... morning
medico, il .... physician
meglio .... better
mela, la (le mele) .... apple
meno .... less, minus
meno un quarto .... a quarter to
menù, il .... menu
mercato, il .... market
mercoledì .... Wednesday
mese, il, (i mesi) .... month
metro, il (i metri) .... meter
metro, la; metropolitana, la .... subway
mezzanotte, la .... midnight
mezzo .... middle
mezzogiorno, il .... noon
mi scusi .... excuse me
mila .... two or more thousand
milione .... million
mille .... one thousand
minestra, la .... soup
minuto, il, (i minuti) .... minute
molto .... very
momento, il .... moment
Un momento! .... Just a moment!
moneta, la .... coin
montagne, le .... mountain
mostrare .... to show
multicolore .... multi-colored
multa .... traffic fine
museo, il .... museum
mutande, le .... underpants

N

nave, la .... ship
neanche .... either
nebbia, la .... fog
necessario .... necessary
negozio, il (i negozi) .... store
nel, nella .... in the
nero .... black
nevica .... it snows
niente .... nothing
nome, il (i nomi) .... name
noi .... we
non .... not, no
nonna, la .... grandmother
nonni, i .... grandparents
nonno, il .... grandfather
nord, il .... north
del nord .... northern
notte, la .... night
novanta .... ninety
nove .... nine
novembre .... November
numero, il (i numeri) .... number
nuova, nuovo .... new

O

o .... or
occhiali, gli .... eyeglasses
occupato .... occupied
oggi .... today
ogni .... each, every
oltrepassa .... goes beyond
ombrello, l' .... umbrella
opera, l' .... opera
operatore, l' .... telephone operator
ora, la (le ore) .... hour
orario, l' .... timetable
ordinare .... to order
orologeria, l' ....
.... clock and watchmaker's shop
l'orologio (gli orologi) .... clock
ospedale, l' .... hospital
ostello della gioventù, l' ... youth hostel
osteria, l' .... cafe
ottanta .... eighty
otto .... eight
ottobre .... October
ovest, l' .... west
dell'ovest .... western

P

padre, il .... father
pagare .... to pay
pagina, la .... page
paio, il .... pair
palazzo, il .... palace
palla, la .... ball
pane, il .... bread
panificio, il .... bakery
pantofole, le .... slippers
pantaloni, i .... trousers
paragrafo, il .... paragraph
parcheggio, il .... parking lot
parco, il .... park
parenti, i .... relatives
parete, la .... wall
parlare .... to speak
parola, la (le parole) .... word
parole crociate .... crossword puzzle
parrucchiere, il .... hairdresser
partenza, la .... departure
partire .... to leave
passaporto, il .... passport
pastasciutta, la .... pasta
pasticceria, la .... pastry shop
pasto, il .... meal
pellicola, la .... film
penna, la .... pen
pepe, il .... pepper
per .... for
per favore, per piacere .... please
perchè .... why
perdere .... to lose
persona, la (le persone) .... person
pesce, il .... fish
pescheria, la .... fish market
pettine, il .... comb
pezzo, il .... piece
piacere, il .... pleasure
per piacere .... if you please
Molto piacere ....
.... "It's a pleasure to meet you."
piano .... softly
piano, il .... floor
pianta, la .... map
pianterreno, il .... ground floor
piatto, il .... plate, dish
la piazza .... plaza, town square
piccolo, piccola .... little
piede, il (i piedi) .... foot
pigiama, il .... pajamas
pila, la .... battery
piove .... it rains
pittura, la .... paint
più .... more
più tardi .... later
poco .... little
poi .... then
polizia, la .... police
pollame, il .... poultry
pomeriggio, il .... afternoon
porta, la .... door
portafoglio, il .... wallet
possibilità, la .... possibility
possono/potere .... can/to be able to
posta, la .... mail, post office
posteggio, il .... parking place
posto, il .... seat
potere .... to be able to/can
povero .... poor
PT, le... .... post office
pranzo, il .... lunch
precedente .... preceding
prego .... you're welcome
premere .... to press
prenda .... take
prenotare .... to reserve/to book
prenotazioni, le .... reservations
prepararmi .... to prepare for me
preposizioni, le .... prepositions
prezzo, il .... price
prima classe, la .... first class
prima colazione, la .... breakfast
primavera, la .... spring
priorità .... yield
profumo, il .... perfume
pronto .... prompt, ready
"Pronto!" ....
.... "Hello!" (when answering telephone)
prosciutto, il .... ham
prossima .... next
protestante .... Protestant
pulito, pulita .... clean
pulsante, il .... push button
può/potere .... can/to be able to

Q

quadro, il .... picture
quale .... what, which
quando .... when
quanto .... how much
quaranta .... forty
quarto, un .... quarter
e un quarto .... a quarter past
meno un quarto .... a quarter to
quattordici .... fourteen
quattro .... four
queste .... these
questo .... this
questura, la .... police station
qui .... here
quindici .... fifteen

R

ragazza, la .... girl
ragazzo, il .... boy
rapido .... rapid, fast
rapido, il .... very fast train
rasoio, il .... razor
reggipetto, il .... brassière
religione, la (le religioni) ...... religion
restare .... to remain, to stay
reparto, il .... department
ricco .... rich
ricevitore, il .... receiver (telephone)
ricevuta, la .... receipt
ripeta/ripetere .... repeat/to repeat
riso, il .... rice
risponda/rispondere . respond/to respond
risposta, la (le risposte) .... answer
ristorante, il .... restaurant

ritardo ... late
rivista, la ... magazine
Roma ... Rome
rosa, la (le rose) ... rose
rosa ... pink
rosso, rossa ... red

S

sabato ... Saturday
sala d'aspetto, la ... waiting room
sala da pranzo, la ... dining room
salata ... salted, salty
sale, il ... salt
Sali e Tabacchi, i . salt and tobacco store
salire ... to board/to climb into
salotto, il ... living room
salsiccia, la ... sausage
salumeria, la ... delicatessen
salumi, i ... sausages, salami
salute, la ... health
saluto, il (i saluti) ... greeting
sandalo, il (i sandali) ... sandal
sangue, il ... blood
sapere .. to know (a fact, an address, etc.)
sapone, il ... soap
sarta, la ... seamstress
sarto, il ... tailor
sbarcare ... to disembark
scala, la (le scale) ... staircase, stairs
la Scala ... Milanese opera house
scala mobile, la ... escalator
scarpa, la (le scarpe) ... shoe
scendere ... to get out/go down
scompartimento, lo ... compartment
scrivania, la ... desk
scrivere ... to write
scuola, la ... school
secco ... dry
seconda ... second
seconda classe, la ... second class
sedia, la ... chair
sedici ... sixteen
seduto ... seated
segnale, il ... signal, sign
segretario, il ... secretary
seguente, seguenti ... following
sei ... six
semplice .. simple, easy, one-way (ticket)
senso unico, il ... one-way street
sera, la ... evening
servizio, il ... service
sessanta ... sixty
settanta ... seventy
sette ... seven
settembre ... September
settimana, la (le settimane) ... week
sí ... yes
signora, la (le signore) ... lady
signore, il (i signori) ... gentleman
simile, simili ... similar
similitudine, la (le similitudini) ... similarity
sinistra ... left
a sinistra ... to the left
sofà, il ... sofa
soffitto, il ... the ceiling
soggetto, il ... subject
solamente ... only
somma, la ... sum
sono ... they are
sopra ... over, above
soprabito, il ... coat
sorella, la ... sister
sorpresa, la ... surprise
sottile ... thin
sotto ... under, below
sottoveste, la ... slip
spazzolino da denti, lo ... toothbrush
specchio, lo ... mirror
specialità, le ... specialities
spesso ... often
spiaggia, la ... beach
sportello, lo ... ticket window
squisito ... delicious
stagioni, le ... seasons
stanco ... tired
stanza, la ... room
stanza da bagno, la ... bathroom
Stati Uniti, gli ... United States
stazione di benzina, la ... gas station
stazione dei treni, la ... train station
stivale, lo (gli stivali) ... boot
strada, la ... street
straniero, lo ... stranger, foreigner
straordinario ... extraordinary
su ... on
Sua, Suo ... your
subito ... immediately
succede ... happening
Che succede? ... What's happening?
succo, il ... juice
succo di arancia, il ... orange juice
succo di pompelmo, il . grapefruit juice
sud, il ... south
del sud ... southern
sugo, il ... sauce
sul, sulla ... on the
supermercato, il ... grocery store
sveglia, la ... alarm clock

T

tabacco, il ... tobacco
taglia, la ... size
tagliano ... cut
tappeto, il ... carpet
tariffa, la ... fare
tassì, il ... taxi
tavolo, il ... table
tavola calda, la ... cafeteria
tazza, la (le tazze) ... cup
tè, il ... tea
teatro, il ... theater
telefono, il ... telephone
telefonata, la ... telephone call
telefonata interurbana, la ... long-distance call
telegramma, il ... telegram
televisore, il ... television
temperatura, la (le temperature) ... temperature
tempo, il ... weather, time
tendina, la ... curtain
termometro, il ... thermometer
tintoria, la ... dry cleaner's
tipico, tipica ... typical
torre, la ... tower
La Torre Pendente ... Leaning Tower of Pisa
tovagliolo, il ... napkin
tram, il ... tram, street car
trattoria, la ... restaurant
trasporto, il ... transportation
tre ... three
tredici ... thirteen
treno, il (i treni) ... train
trenta ... thirty
trovare ... to find
turista, il ... tourist
tutto ... everything

U

ufficio, l' ... office
ufficio oggetti smarriti ... lost-and-found office
ufficio di cambio, l' ... money-exchange office
ufficio deposito bagagli, l' ... left-luggage office
ufficio informazioni ... information office
ufficio postale italiano, l' ... post office
un, un', una, uno ... a
undici ... eleven
unico ... unique, only, single
senso unico ... one-way (traffic sign)
università, l' ... university
uno ... one
uomo, l' (gli uomini) ... man
uova, le ... eggs
uova affogate, le ... poached egg
uova fritte, le ... fried egg
uova strapazzate, le ... scrambled egg
uscire ... to go out
uscita, l' ... exit
uscita principale, l' ... main exit
uscita di sicurezza, l' .. emergency exit
usuale ... usual, customary

V

vacanze, le ... vacation
fare le vacanze ... to take a vacation
vada/andare ... go/to go
vagone letto, il ... sleeping car
vagone ristorante, il ... dining car
valigia, la ... suitcase
vaniglia, la ... vanilla
vaso, il ... vase
vecchia, vecchio ... old
vedere ... to see
veloce ... fast
vendere ... to sell
venditore, il ... vendor, seller
venerdì ... Friday
venire ... to come
venti ... twenty
vento, il ... windy
tira vento ... it's windy
verbo, il (i verbi) ... verb
verde ... green
verdure, le ... vegetables
vestiti, i ... clothing
vestito, il ... dress
via ... by
via, la ... way
via aerea ... air mail
viaggia ... travel, travels
viaggiatore, il ... traveler
viaggio, il ... trip
vicino ... near
viene/venire ... come, comes/to come
vietato ... prohibited
vietato l'ingresso ... do not enter
vigoroso ... vigorous
vino, il ... wine
vino della casa, il ... house wine
violetto ... violet
visita, la ... visit
fare una visita ... to pay a visit
vitello, il ... veal
volare ... to fly/go by plane
volere ... would like
volo, il ... flight
vorrei/volere ... I would like/would like
vorremmo/volere ... we would like/would like

W

W.C., il ... water closet

Z

zaino, lo ... backpack
zero, lo ... zero
zia, la ... aunt
zio, lo ... uncle
zoo, lo ... zoo
zuppa, la (le zuppe) ... soup

DRINKING GUIDE

This guide is intended to explain the sometimes overwhelming variety of beverages available to you while in Italy. It is by no means complete. Some of the experimenting has been left up to you, but this should get you started. The asterisks (*) indicate brand names.

BEVANDE CALDE (hot drinks)

caffè (espresso) .... espresso coffee
caffelatte .... coffee with milk
cappuccino .... coffee topped with steamed milk
caffè macchiato .... coffee with a little milk or cream
caffè americano .... American coffee
tè .... tea
con limone .... with lemon
con latte .... with milk
cioccolata .... hot chocolate

BEVANDE FREDDE (cold drinks)

latte freddo .... cold milk
frappé .... milk shake
acqua minerale .... mineral water
***San Pellegrino**
***Recoaro**
***Montecatini**
aranciata .... orangeade
limonata .... lemon drink
spremuta di limone .... lemonade
succo di frutta .... fruit juice
amarena .... cherry syrup drink
orzata .... almond syrup drink
gassosa .... carbonated soft drink
tè freddo .... iced tea
caffè freddo .... iced coffee

APERITIVI (aperitifs) These may be enjoyed straight or over ice.

sherry .... sherry
porto .... port
***Martini bianco** .... white vermouth
***Martini rosso** .... red vermouth
***Pernod** .... anise base
***Campari**
***Cinzano**
***Punt e Mes**

BIRRE (beers) There is not a great variety of beers in Italy. **La birra** is purchased in **bottiglia** (bottle).

***Peroni**
***Italia**

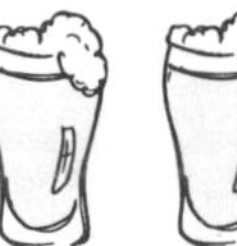

IL GHIACCIO .... ice

VINI (wines) There is a very wide variety of wines in Italy and you will want to try many of them. Each region produces its own wine, ranging in taste from very sweet to very dry. You may drink wine by the **bicchiere** (glass), **litro** (liter), **mezzo litro** (half liter) or the **bottiglia** (bottle).

vino rosso .... red wine
vino bianco .... white wine
vino rosè .... rosè wine
spumante .... sparkling wine
vino ordinario .... table wine
vino da tavola .... table wine
vino della casa .... house wine
vino locale .... local wine of the region
dolce .... sweet
amabile .... between sweet and dry
secco .... dry

WINE	REGION	COLOR	TASTE
***Barbera**	**Emilia**	**rosso**	**secco/amabile**
***Barolo**	**Piemonte**	**rosso**	**secco**
***Chianti**	**Toscana**	**rosso**	**secco**
***Lambrusco**	**Emilia**	**rosso**	**secco/amabile**
***Verdicchio**	**le Marche**	**bianco**	**secco**
marsala siciliano	**Sicilia**	**rosso**	**dolce**
moscato	**Toscana**	**bianco**	**dolce**

ALCOOL (spirits) Cocktail drinking is not widespread in Italy. The following are available in large, international hotels and **"bar americani."**

gin .... gin
bourbon .... bourbon
rum .... rum
vodka .... vodka
whisky .... scotch
martini dry .... American martini

DIGESTIVI (liqueurs, brandies)

acquavite .... natural grain spirits
grappa .... wine brandy
***Fernet-Branca** .... herb base
***Alpestre** .... herb base
***Ferro China** .... bark base
***Amaretto** .... almond base
***Sambuca** .... anise base
con la mosca .... with a coffee bean
***Drambuie**
***Cointreau**
***Grand Marnier**

CUT ALONG DOTTED LINE, FOLD AND TAKE WITH YOU

Pesci e Frutti di Mare (fish and seafood)

acciughe	anchovies
anguilla	eel
aragosta	lobster
calamari	squid
cefalo	gray mullet
gamberi	shrimp or prawns
granchio	crab
merluzzo	codfish
muscoli	mussels
persico	perch
pesce spada	swordfish
polipo	octopus
rane	frogs
salmone	salmon
sardine	sardines
sogliola	sole
spigola	sea bass
storione	sturgeon
tonno	tuna
triglie	red mullet
trota	trout
vongole	clams

Verdure (vegetables)

cipolle	onions
piselli	green peas
pomodori	tomatoes
fagiolini	string beans
cavolfiore	cauliflower
carciofo	artichokes
carote	carrots
asparagi	asparagus
spinaci	spinach
lenticchie	lentils
funghi	mushrooms
broccoli	broccoli
finocchio	fennel
melanzane	eggplant
olive	olives
patate	potatoes
peperoni	bell peppers
porri	leeks
prezzemolo	parsley
rapanelli	radishes
sedano	celery
zucca	yellow squash
zucchini	zucchini
misto di verdure	mixed cooked vegetables

FOLD HERE

Insalata (salad)

verde	tossed green salad
capricciosa	mixed vegetables, with ham in mayonnaise sauce
di pesce	boiled fish
di riso	cold rice, vegetables, seafood, mayonnaise
russa	vegetables, hard-boiled eggs, mayonnaise
viennese	tuna, hard-boiled eggs, beans, olives

Riso, Risotto (rice)

alla milanese	with saffron
con funghi	with mushrooms
alla marinara	tomato sauce, clams, prawns
Risi e Bisi	rice and peas
Supplì	deep-fried rice balls

Frutta (fruit)

mela	apple
pera	pear
albicocca	apricot
pesca	peach
banana	banana
arancia	orange
mandarino	tangerine
ciliege	cherries
cocomero	watermelon
prugna	plum
uva	grapes
uva passa	raisins
dattero	date
noce di cocco	coconut
limone	lemon
ananas	pineapple
pompelmo	grapefruit
fichi	figs
fragole	strawberries
lamponi	raspberries
mirtilli	blueberries
macedonia di frutta	fruit salad
misto bosco	mixed berries

Buon appetito!

FOLD HERE

Il Menu

Preparazione (preparation)

cotto	cooked
crudo	raw
arrosto	roast
fritto	fried
al forno	baked
alla griglia, ai ferri	grilled
allo spiedo	roasted on a spit
bollito	boiled
affumicato	smoked
alla brace	charcoal-broiled
farcito	stuffed
al sangue	rare
al punto	medium
ben cotto	well-done

Altri (others)

marmellata	jam
miele	honey
sale	salt
pepe	pepper
olio	oil
aceto	vinegar
senape/mostarda	mustard
riso	rice
pane	bread
formaggio	cheese
dolci	pastry and dessert
torta	cake
dolce	pastry
gelato	ice cream
panna montata	whipped cream

Antipasti (appetizers)

acciughe — anchovies
di mare — seafood with lemon-juice dressing
misto — mixed appetizers
bagna cauda — raw vegetables dipped in dressing
frutti di mare — seafood
gamberi — shrimps and prawns
lumache — snails
ostriche — oysters
peperonata — sliced peppers, onions and tomatoes
mortadella — bologna
polipo — octopus
porchetta romana — stuffed pig
prosciutto — ham
salame — variety of sausages
salsicce — cooked sausage
tartufi — truffles

Minestre e Zuppe (soups)

minestrone — thick vegetable soup
minestrina — thin clear broth
zuppa di pesce — fish soup
brodo — broth
stracciatella — broth with beaten eggs and Parmesan
pavese — broth with poached egg on fried bread

Pastasciutta (pasta)

spaghetti — long, solid-core pasta
fettucine — flat noodle
ravioli — stuffed pasta, small and usually square
lasagne — baked, layered casserole
cannelloni — stuffed cylinder-shaped pasta
tortellini — small stuffed pasta, often in soups
vermicelli — very thin pasta
cannolo — short tubes of macaroni
cappelletti — round, cap-shaped pasta
conchiglie — shell-shaped pasta
farfallette — butterfly-shaped pasta
fusilli — spiral-shaped pasta
gnocchi — small dumpling
linguine — narrow, flat noodles
penne — hollow pasta, cut diagonally
rigatoni — large, hollow pasta

FOLD HERE

Sugo di Carne (meat sauces)

alla bolognese — meat sauce used most often in America
alla romagnola — tomato sauce with garlic and parsley
alla carbonara — sauce of eggs, bacon and garlic
alla fiorentina — herbal meat sauce with green peas
all'arrabbiata — herbal tomato sauce of bacon,sausage and cayenne
alla piemontese — herbal meat sauce with nutmeg and truffles
alla romana — seasoned meat sauce

Senza Carne (meatless sauces)

aglio e olio — olive oil and garlic
alla besciamella — creamed white sauce
al burro — butter and Parmesan
alla Campagnola — mushrooms, tomatoes and herbs
alla Crema — white sauce with egg yolk and Parmesan
alla Genovese — basil, garlic and pine nuts
alla Napolitana — tomatoes, basil and Parmesan
al Pomodoro — herbal tomato sauce

Frutti di Mare (seafood sauces)

alla Boscaiola — tuna, anchovies, tomatoes, and mushrooms
ai Frutti di Mare — herbs, tomatoes and seafoods
al Tonno — tuna, garlic, tomatoes and capers
di Magro — tuna, anchovies and herbs
alla Posillipo — herbs, tomatoes and seafood
alle Vongole — clams and garlic, with or without tomatoes

Carne (meat)

Cacciagione (wild game)

anitra — duck
cervo — deer
coniglio — rabbit
lepre — hare
tordo — thrush

FOLD HERE

Pollame (poultry)

pollo, gallina — chicken
tacchino — turkey
faraona — guinea fowl
cappone — capon
piccione — pigeon
quaglie — quail
fagiano — pheasant

Vitello (veal)

bianchette di vitello — veal stew with gravy
bistecca di vitello — loin veal steak
costoletta di vitello — veal chop or steak
coteletta — veal steak without bone
alla Milanese — breaded veal cutlets
lombata di vitello — loin of veal
lingua di vitello — tongue
noce di vitello — sirloin of veal
rollatine di vitello — rolled stuffed breast of veal
spalla di vitello al forno — roast shoulder of veal
rognone di vitello — kidney

Agnello (lamb)

abbacchio — milk-fed lamb
braciolette d'abbacchio — grilled lamb chops or cutlets
abbacchio al forno — roasted lamb
costole alla Milanese — fried breaded lamb chops
tracciole d'agnello — like shish kebab

Manzo (beef)

bistecca alla Fiorentina — unboned rib steak
braciole — rib steak
entrecote — boneless rib steak
fegato — liver
cervella — brains
lingua di bue — beef tongue
stracotto — stew
trippe — tripe

Maiale (pork)

arista di maiale — roast loin of pork
arrostino alla salvia — roast pork with sage
arrosto di porchetta — stuffed roast suckling pig
zampe di maiale — pig's feet

(veh-nee-reh) **venire**	*(kee-ah-mahr-see)* **chiamarsi**
(ahn-dah-reh) **andare**	*(kohm-prah-reh)* **comprare**
(ah-veh-reh) **avere**	*(pahr-lah-reh)* **parlare**
(eem-pah-rah-reh) **imparare**	*(ah-bee-tah-reh)* **abitare**
(voh-reh-ee) **vorrei**	*(ohr-dee-nah-reh)* **ordinare**
(ah-veh-reh) (bee-sohn-yoh) (dee) **avere bisogno di**	*(reh-stah-reh)* **restare**

to be called

to come

to buy

to go

to speak

to have

to live/reside

to learn

to order

I would like

to stay/remain

to need

(dee-reh) **dire**	*(vehn-deh-reh)* **vendere**
(mahn-jah-reh) **mangiare**	*(veh-deh-reh)* **vedere**
(beh-reh) **bere**	*(mahn-dah-reh)* **mandare**
(ah-spet-tah-reh) **aspettare**	*(dohr-mee-reh)* **dormire**
(kah-pee-reh) **capire**	*(troh-vah-reh)* **trovare**
(ree-peh-teh-reh) **ripetere**	*(fah-reh)* **fare**

to sell	to say
to see	to eat
to send	to drink
to sleep	to wait
to find	to understand
to do/make	to repeat

(skree-veh-reh) **scrivere**	*(leh-jeh-reh)* **leggere**
(moh-strah-reh) **mostrare**	*(vee-ah-jah-reh)* **viaggiare**
(pah-gah-reh) **pagare**	*(lah-voh-rah-reh)* **lavorare**
(poh-teh-reh) **potere**	*(ahn-dah-reh) (een) (ah-air-ree-oh)* **andare in aereo**
(doh-veh-reh) **dovere**	*(chee) (voo-oh-leh) (vohl-yoh-noh)* **ci vuole/ci vogliono**
(sah-peh-reh) **sapere**	*(fah-reh) (lah) (vah-lee-jah)* **fare la valigia**

to read	to write
to travel	to show
to work	to pay
to fly/go by plane	to be able to/can
it takes	to have to/must/owe
to pack	to know

(pahr-tee-reh) **partire**	*(kee-oo-deh-reh)* **chiudere**
(gwee-dah-reh) **guidare**	*(lah-vah-reh)* **lavare**
(foo-mah-reh) **fumare**	*(kahm-bee-ah-reh)* **cambiare**
(doh-mahn-dah-reh) **domandare**	*(pehr-deh-reh)* **perdere**
(neh-vee-kah) **nevica**	*(ee-oh) (soh-noh)* **(io) sono**
(pee-oh-veh) **piove**	*(noh-ee) (see-ah-moh)* **(noi) siamo**

to close	to depart/leave
to wash	to drive
to exchange/change	to smoke
to lose	to ask
I am	it is snowing
we are	it is raining

(een-koh-meen-chah-reh) **incominciare**	*(prehn-deh-reh)* **prendere**
(ah-pree-reh) **aprire**	*(sah-lee-reh)* **salire**
(koo-chee-nah-reh) **cucinare**	*(shen-deh-reh)* **scendere**
(aht-tehr-rah-reh) **atterrare**	*(en-trah-reh)* **entrare**
(preh-noh-tah-reh) **prenotare**	*(kahm-bee-ah-reh)* **cambiare**
(koh-stah-reh) **costare**	*(ahr-ree-vah-reh)* **arrivare**

to take

to climb/board

to go down/get out

to enter

to transfer

to arrive

to begin

to open

to cook

to land

to book/reserve

to cost

(bwoh-noh) (kaht-tee-voh)
buono - cattivo

(veh-loh-cheh) (rah-pee-doh) (len-toh)
veloce/rapido - lento

(pee-ah-noh) (fohr-teh)
piano - forte

(grohs-soh) (soht-tee-leh)
grosso - sottile

(grahn-deh) (peek-koh-loh)
grande - piccolo

(mohl-toh) (poh-koh)
molto - poco

(kahl-doh) (frehd-doh)
caldo - freddo

(ah-pehr-toh) (kee-oo-soh)
aperto - chiuso

(see-nee-strah) (deh-strah)
sinistra - destra

(dohl-cheh) (ah-groh)
dolce - agro

(soh-prah) (soht-toh)
sopra - sotto

(mee) (skoo-see) (pehr-mess-soh)
mi scusi - permesso

fast - slow	good - bad
thick - thin	soft - loud
much - little	large - small
open - closed	warm - cold
sweet - sour	left - right
excuse me	above - below

(loo-ee) **lui** / (leh-ee) **lei** } **è**	(ahl-toh) (bahs-soh) **alto - basso**
(leh-ee) (eh) **Lei è**	(poh-veh-roh) (reek-koh) **povero - ricco**
(loh-roh) (soh-noh) **loro sono**	(kohr-toh) (loon-goh) **corto - lungo**
(ahr-ree-veh-dehr-chee) **arrivederci**	(mah-lah-toh) **malato -** (dee) (bwoh-nah) (sah-loo-teh) **di buona salute**
(cheh) (chee) (soh-noh) **c'è / ci sono**	(eh-koh-noh-mee-koh) (kah-roh) **economico - caro**
(koh-meh) (vah) **Come va?**	(vek-kee-oh) (joh-vah-neh) **vecchio - giovane**

high - low	he } is she }
poor - rich	you are
short - long	they are
sick - healthy	good-bye
cheap - expensive	there is/there are
old - young	How are you?

Now that you've finished . . .

You've done it!

You've completed all 23 Steps, stuck your labels, flashed your cards and clipped your menu. Do you realize how far you've come and how much you've learned? In a short period of time, you have accomplished what it sometimes takes years to achieve in a traditional language class.

You can now confidently

- ask questions,
- understand directions,
- make reservations,
- order food and
- shop anywhere.

And you can do it all in a foreign language! This means you can now go anywhere – from a large cosmopolitan restaurant to a small, out-of-the-way village where no one speaks English. Your experiences will be much more enjoyable and worry-free now that you speak the language, understand what is being said and know something of the culture.

Yes, learning a foreign language can be fun. And no, not everyone abroad speaks English.

Kristine Kershul

Have a wonderful time, whether your trip is to Europe, the Orient or simply across the border.

REORDER FORM

Title	Quantity	Price/book	Total
Chinese		US $15.99	
French		US $15.99	
German		US $15.99	
Hebrew		US $15.99	
Inglés		US $15.99	
Italian		US $15.99	
Japanese		US $15.99	
Norwegian		US $15.99	
Russian		US $15.99	
Spanish		US $15.99	
		Shipping*	
		WA residents add tax	
		Total Order	

*In the US add $4 for the first book and $1 for each additional book. On foreign orders add $8 for the first book and $4 for each additional book for airmail shipment.

Please Check:

☐ Bill my credit card account ☐ VISA ☐ MC

No.____________________ Exp.date ___/___

☐ My check for $________________ is enclosed.

Name____________________

Address____________________

City________________ State____ Zip______

Telephone No.(______)________________

Signature____________________

REORDER FORM

Title	Quantity	Price/book	Total
Chinese		US $15.99	
French		US $15.99	
German		US $15.99	
Hebrew		US $15.99	
Inglés		US $15.99	
Italian		US $15.99	
Japanese		US $15.99	
Norwegian		US $15.99	
Russian		US $15.99	
Spanish		US $15.99	
		Shipping*	
		WA residents add tax	
		Total Order	

*In the US add $4 for the first book and $1 for each additional book. On foreign orders add $8 for the first book and $4 for each additional book for airmail shipment.

Please Check:

☐ Bill my credit card account ☐ VISA ☐ MC

No.____________________ Exp.date ___/___

☐ My check for $________________ is enclosed.

Name____________________

Address____________________

City________________ State____ Zip______

Telephone No.(______)________________

Signature____________________

BUSINESS REPLY MAIL
FIRST CLASS MAIL PERMIT NO. 8300 SEATTLE, WA

POSTAGE WILL BE PAID BY ADDRESSEE

BILINGUAL BOOKS INC.
511 EASTLAKE AVENUE EAST
SEATTLE, WA 98109 - 9946

NO POSTAGE NECESSARY IF MAILED IN THE UNITED STATES

BUSINESS REPLY MAIL
FIRST CLASS MAIL PERMIT NO. 8300 SEATTLE, WA

POSTAGE WILL BE PAID BY ADDRESEE

BILINGUAL BOOKS INC.
511 EASTLAKE AVENUE EAST
SEATTLE, WA 98109 - 9946

NO POSTAGE NECESSARY IF MAILED IN THE UNITED STATES

Thank you!

More than two million copies of the ***10 minutes a day***® series have been sold worldwide. We are pleased to have you join the many travelers, students and business people who have successfully – and enjoyably – learned another language in just ***10 minutes a day***®!

At Bilingual Books, we are constantly looking for ways to improve our books, to offer you even greater value and to make your foreign language learning experience easy, fun and effective.

Please tell us how we can serve you better. Would you like a CD-ROM supplement for your computer? Audio tapes for the commute to work or school? New languages?

Let us know what you would like to see available in this series and, above all, send us a postcard from your travels. Or better yet, send us a picture of you at the Eiffel Tower, the Great Wall of China, the beach in Mexico, or from your favorite restaurant in Italy. Share with us how you got along with your new language skills, what you truly enjoyed on your trip and where you plan to travel next!

Here's our new address and telephone number:

Bilingual Books Inc.
511 Eastlake Avenue East
Seattle, WA 98109 USA
(206) 340-4422